NEVER COUNT CROW

love and loss in Kennebunk, Maine

CYNTHIA FRASER GRAVES

Bloomington, IN Milton Keynes, UK

authorHOUSE®

AuthorHouse™
1663 Liberty Drive, Suite 200
Bloomington, IN 47403
www.authorhouse.com
Phone: 1-800-839-8640

AuthorHouse™ UK Ltd.
500 Avebury Boulevard
Central Milton Keynes, MK9 2BE
www.authorhouse.co.uk
Phone: 08001974150

First published by AuthorHouse 11/29/2006

ISBN: 978-1-4259-6603-4 (sc)

Printed in the United States of America
Bloomington, Indiana

This book is printed on acid-free paper.

Many thanks to those wonderful friends who were there to support me on my way with hours of reading and encouragement: to Meredith Jordan; John and Paulette Forssen; my brother, Ted Fraser; Pat Walsh; Monica Fraser; the Prayer Group of St. Christopher's Church in Hobe Sound, Florida; Bette Simmons; Pat Preputin; my daughter, Rebecca Graves; and Dominic, my partner.

Without these people, *Never Count Crow* could not have found its way into print.

For Rebecca, Eben, and Osman

loss

how will I hear you
when you speak to me?

will your voice be in
the croaking call of crows
spiraling on gray winds
to high-perched oaks?

will your words descend in silence,
crushing though unpronounced,
striking at the core, and
bring me to cracked pavement
beneath bent knees?

when you speak,
will your voice be wind,
cool dark wind
brushing the quiet grass
of night?

will you suddenly call
through the copse of small trees
in some woods as
I walk past,
wanting to be known?

or

will your words,
like waves,
dissolve,
each into each,
until no one
word
remains,
and you
are lost
to me.

CYNTHIA FRASER GRAVES

"I have sent you nothing but angels."

A COURSE IN MIRACLES

"O smiling angel, sympathetic stone
with mouth as from a hundred mouths distilled:
do you not mark how, from your ever-filled
sundial, our hours are gliding one by one-"

RAINER MARIA RILKE

"You are Polaris, the one trustworthy star, you are, you are..."

METAPHOR, THE FANTASTICKS

NEVER COUNT CROW

1972

"One crow, sorrow; two crows, joy; three crows, a letter; four crows, a boy; five crows, silver; six crows, gold; seven crows, a story that is going to be told."

Marion Graves, or Nanny, as she had my children call her, first counted the round of crows years ago. I see her installed like a Buddha, head turbaned in the smoke drifting from her cigarette. Her living room was always the same in the many houses she bought and sold. As the first woman in real estate in Marblehead, Massachusetts, she kept her professional skills honed in retirement by becoming a frequent customer in the realtor's office. Her interchangeable habitats consistently turned out to be cream colored, with long, narrow parlors, no matter what the shape when purchased.

The windows in the house were always bare, the scenery being more important than the convention of drapes or curtains. On a round, gilt-painted coffee table was a bouquet that changed on each solstice. In winter, it was a pine branch with pine cones and holly berries; in summer and spring, single flowers of cosmos, a rose, or chrysanthemums; in fall, a branch of autumn leaves wound with bittersweet. These bouquets sprouted from a narrow-necked green bottle that I inherited at her death and that I lived to see drop and smash on the floor of my house on Pleasant Street.

Sometimes, when I turn suddenly, the bottle still stands on the time-dulled coffee table that I inherited.

Nanny's furniture was eclectic, but permanent. Most of it reflected the woodsy style she loved. She and Sid, my father-in-law, moved to Andover, Maine, in search of the rustic northern New England life and plainness of style that the region seemed to offer, in contrast to the dictated and obligatory social patterns they had lived for most of their lives in Marblehead, Massachusetts. The existence they left behind in Marblehead was laced with the Baptist's dim view of fun. Sid often told of dull Sundays in his youth, when playing ball, reading, or laughing was not allowed. All this misery was inflicted on a man who was a comedian at heart and ended up playing good baseball for the Braves. These rigid behaviors were signs of Puritan good breeding and were expectations the gentry in these old towns held onto like flotation devices.

On some tabletop or wall in one of the main rooms of her house, there was always the picture of Marion, more familiar as Nanny, beside a six-point buck that she had allegedly brought down. She encouraged this image and played the rebel in her way, often dressing in plaid wool shirts and carrying a gun around in her car during hunting season. This was her way of sailing in the face of the rigid gentility she found so suffocating in Massachusetts. Moving to Maine allowed her to include some of her authentic self in her public face. There was some evidence in whispers and winks that the picture of Marion standing over the buck might have been staged. I never did find out for sure.

The first thing she and Sid would do in any house, and they changed houses three times in Kennebunk alone, was to have a large, walk-in fireplace built, preferably out of rough fieldstone. Winter nights would feel fierce fires blaze away the cold. They would strip the floors of any carpets or tile and refinish the exposed wood in light tones, shellacking them to a "high-heaven" shine. The blazing fires on the large hearth would light the floors up and the house would glow. In this sparkling court, cigarette holder in hand, feet up on an ottoman, Nanny would preside over dinner and conversation.

Looking to instill awe in the participants on these evenings, she chanted the Crow verses. "One crow, sorrow; two crows, joy; three crows, a letter; four crows, a boy; five crows, silver; six crows, gold; seven crows, a story that is going to be told," Her throaty voice sang in the firelight.

"Just a saying from my folks up in Malone, New York, though I've seen it to be so many times myself. Counting crow was taken as Bible truth by my grandparents and my parents, too. They wouldn't look at a single crow for love nor money."

She would direct me to sit at her feet, and I, the impressionable new wife to her only son, and later, new mother with a tender baby girl on my lap, heard wisdom dressed in black feathers. The chant hovered in the flickering light, a litany binding real events with the mystical, and settled around my heart, a charm against whatever evil might be contained in the dim corners of that day. What did I know then of sorrow, as I was just starting out with my little family gathered close at the end of each day? What could I have seen in the custom but a curious artifact of tradition? How could I have known then how this ritual would echo in the events that already waited ahead?

The intervening years have taught me to pay attention to the seemingly unconnected world of simple, everyday events. I have come lately to know my life as the gift it is, priceless in light of the swiftly passing events I could never have imagined on those evenings as Nanny initiated me into the counting of crows.

Crows and their gatherings became part of the language and imagery of our growing family of four. By 1980, I had left the ranks of mothers-at-home and was teaching Language Arts in a nearby middle school. Often, as I rushed to work on the Maine Turnpike—still an empty ribbon of road in those early hours, where now, three lanes of traffic flow constantly—I would scout for black clouds of crows lifting into the morning winds. Would one crow swoop ominously toward me? How many could I count, and if there was only one crow to be found, how long could I wait before counting it? Would even noticing the iconic bird constitute "counting" it? It was simply a diversion, a game; but a game that always mattered. In addition to the black talisman during my morning musings, I made the acquaintance of owls and hawks. They watched me as keenly as I watched them. The common task of traveling to and from school became an odyssey through the rapt attention they lavished on me. There was one owl I felt on familiar terms with.

> *An ancient owl turns his yellow eyes on me*
> *from the ghostly apple tree at exit three,*
> *he beckons from his perch, as*
> *a hawk hovers in my slipstream,*
> *his talons sink into my heart*
> *and the tollbooth rises in the windshield…*

Just behind the shade of the ordinary, something rippled in the air. I heard the whisper of warning; it was received and noted, recorded in the lines of poetry that became insistent and mysterious;

> *precious death is waiting,*
> *as a marble seraph she appears,*
> *poised, mouth open in greeting,*
> *cold robes flowing in a secret breeze.*

not anxious yet,
she points to a silent bell
soon to strike
and release her,
then she will fly to my side.

I did not know to ask then, but I ask now: When does a person's death begin its approach in a palpable way? The appointment is made, the clock is advancing, though we are unaware of its progress. Death will not be denied. It is the remarkable person who, rising to a day full of life plans, scans the skies, seeing the dark cloud forming on the horizon.

We had a death; the most brutal kind, when there is no time for goodbyes, and the absence of the loved one is deep enough to drown in; a death that walked out from behind the scrim of the day that was July14, 1994, a death that stunned our family, and from which we almost didn't recover; a death on Pleasant Street, in the ordinary little village of Kennebunk, Maine.

ferryman, ferryman

pleasant street curves
up and away from town,
following the moon print of
rivers from the past,
rising to a ridge
and flowing out in stealth
toward
the sea.

beneath,
flowing with the asphalt

runs a shadow river,
silent and cold coursing,
secret as a new moon,
and
the ferryman mounts his bark
though
no one marks his departure.

Early morning, 1989

Light rises out of the earth in the little New England town. On a hill overlooking Portland Road, orderly rows of the deceased, laid to rest in Hope Cemetery, become more clearly defined in the rising tide of light. Recently, on a rainy afternoon, some of the townsfolk conducted an interpretive tour of the cemetery, a much-advertised diversion. Guides and their groups walked the darkening avenues, carrying candle-lit lanterns in a gentle rain. The interpreters stopped at various graves and related the lives and affairs of those resting there, now past caring. I walked with them, and when we came to the grave whose story I knew and repeated with every beat of my heart, I moved by without comment. The stories lying silent and forgiven on that hill are many. This tale is just one, but it is mine to tell.

On a morning in 1989, further south along the main street of town, the sun is just rising in the tall windows of an 1881 farmhouse. The house is on the left side of Pleasant Street, a small byway that curves up a gradual hill to the right of Portland Road, now known as Route One. It is an early autumn morning; dry leaves have begun their scuttling down the street, sounding the unmistakable herald of endings: the end of warmth, of summer, and of the hours of freedom from schedules, and if you listen carefully, it sounds the echo of some deeper and more elusive conclusion.

leaf history

scratching its history
across the morning street
like an ancient hand,
the leaf announces
time's shift.

why will it rise out
of silence
staying
in my mind these
various years.

seeing it only as
a late summer day,
we rose and played
at our seriousness,
dressed and rushed,
and completed
what we thought essential
then.

but, yesterday,
in a falling dusk,
the sound came
again
from silence, and
I woke with him,
now quiet beyond belief.

the windows are still
August-wide.
air sings
the same old song,
telling of
love
dressed in blood.

It is August. Gene and I stir with the rise of breeze skimming the river that flows lazily at the foot of our street and spills down the falls in the center of town. Curtains billow softly. Our conversation begins in murmurs settled deep into the large bed centered with its back to the river. This territory is perfectly known to us. We can predict the day's probabilities from the first few moments of wakefulness. We are firmly rooted in the comfortable routines of the twenty years our marriage has counted.

Consciousness continues to gain ground. Gene's eyes flutter open as a surprised hum escapes from him. He has had a dream, one that might just measure up to my rigorous standards. I am the heavyweight intuitive of the family; the bonded visionary. The stories of my initiation to the position are well known in the family circle. It is the story of a little girl coming home from ice skating on a dark, winter evening in Rumford, Maine. Walking along Spruce Street, I am looking forward to a hot dinner and the half-read Nancy Drew mystery that waits for me. As I peer down the long tunnel of that cold, dark street with immense snow banks, at least six feet high on either side of me, I see nothing beyond my wish for food and warmth.

Suddenly, a voice booms out of the dark sky: "Climb the snow bank!" The command is loud and direct. It ripples in the dark air. I stop in my progress and turn a full circle in the utterly empty night street, searching for the speaker. There is no one anywhere in sight, and this deepens my wonder about where the voice came from, and just why I would climb over the snow bank.

At that exact moment, a car comes into sight at the furthest end of Spruce Street. Its lights reach for me up the street, connecting us in the dark air. Again, the commanding voice booms out of the night: "Climb the snow bank!" A bit of fear drives its spear into my heart. I feel exposed, alone, and unsure. Steadily advancing toward me, the car has come halfway up the street. It now looms between me and my front porch. I can see its silhouette in the light my mother has lit to guide me home. It cuts me off from my destination. I do not yet notice that the car is weaving as it proceeds; first one lane, now another. It is only in retrospect that I see the dizzy progress up the little street.

The voice repeats the command once more. This time, because I am a compliant girl, well-trained to obey, I mind the voice. I hesitate no more, but scramble up the snow bank, pulling myself frantically, unreasonably, on chunks of ice to the very top, where I sit and tremble.

The whole bank shudders with the impact of the car as it rams into the frozen snow just below my precarious perch. I watch in silence as the driver gears awkwardly, and the car spins its wheels and lurches stupidly in the road until it gains some direction and balance and weaves down the still-empty street.

I am now shivering in fear. It is almost impossible for my ten-year-old mind to comprehend what has happened. And what interpretation do I finally arrange? The conclusion I draw is that the driver of the car saw me run to the top of the banking and decided to slam in, just under my seat, to show me how childishly I have behaved. It will take many years for me to understand that my life has been saved this night; I do not believe I am important enough for any intervention on my behalf. When, years later, I finally come to realize the truth written in the events of this night,

I feel the sweet touch of a loving mystery and it moves me to a higher ground of knowing.

Another episode began with a conference I attended in Orono, early in my marriage to Gene. He always encouraged me to get away from my routine with house and children and to keep my connection with my profession as a teacher current. Because it was a weekend, he would be home to take my place in the busy life.

Just after breakfast, I am walking down a steep hill to deliver a talk on the use of trade books in teaching adults the basics of plot, character, setting, and theme. Within the space of a second, the solid, recognizable world simply drops away, and I am floating in some dimension I have never experienced before, though I am still on that sidewalk. I don't know how I have arrived in this place. Even though I am still bound by my body, my sight sweeps all of creation in a single glance. I see the shining energy of love rippling beneath the surface of all the particularizations of person and place on the planet.

And I can see Gene, home in our kitchen, taking care of Rebecca and Eben. Their games around the kitchen table are going on and it is as if I am there in the flesh. I know that whatever is happening, it is all perfect, just as it is. A sense of joy and peace rises in me, so powerful that I can't contain it. I become air myself, and glide in rapture down the rest of the hill.

A few minutes later, I arrive to lead the class I have been asked to prepare and break into tears of gratitude just to see the people before me. I'm sure that some of them still remember the very strange instructor at a conference they attended at UMO who wept throughout her presentation. I have no idea what I said; I know only that I disappointed the person who had engaged me to lead the class in the first place as she was observing the proceedings.

On the ride home, I travel above the car in a mist of all-encompassing peace. When I am dropped off at our home in

Kennebunk, then on Storer Street, it feels like walking into a shrine; so holy is the life within those walls. Time dulls the event in my memory, but sharing it brings it back. These and other events have given me my patina of exalted one in Gene's eye's, and are the reason that morning for his delight that he had finally had *his* dream of mystical heft.

He begins to relate the dream, naming it "The Marblehead Boys Speak." It is a dream within a dream, he says; I listen with my eyes still closed, again, unaware of the approach of prediction, and playing the roll of the resident authority waiting to be convinced.

"They were all there: my father, Uncle Leon, and Uncle Joe," Gene relates. "In the dream, I already know they are dead, and I know I am in some place where this meeting is possible, but only for a short time, so I feel like I have to get right to the point. I'm so glad to see them and to see that they are still as I remember them, only a little younger. They are perfect; hair smooth, in dark suits and smiling, really happy. And they are smoking cigars, just looking around and smiling, as if it is really nice to be there."

These dear men, in life, were passionate Marbleheaders who knew the special language and rituals of the old Massachusetts sea community and considered them sacred. "Down bucket, up for air," an arcane greeting used only by and for Marbleheaders, crossed their lips often. Strict Baptists all in their youth, the Graves brothers shared a no-nonsense attitude toward life, and to have them show up all together in one dream in our bedroom on Pleasant Street in Kennebunk was no less than compelling.

Best friends in their lives, they took every opportunity to escape their overbearing wives for time spent together. They all owned black limousines in the Massachusetts tradition and found great delight in escaping into them, cigars burning bright, driving around for hours, talking about how the world was going to hell in the liberals' basket. As the hours collected, the sedan would seemingly glide through the streets of town, a smoke-filled vehicle with no visible occupants.

Gene's father, Sid, a true eccentric, was already a Kennebunk legend for getting himself locked in the freezer of the local supermarket where he was abandoned at closing time. If Marion had been less vigilant for his return and neglected to spread the alarm, morning would have found him frozen. It was written up at the time in the *York County Coast Star*, back when simpler things were still considered news, and when stores actually closed at night.

Gene continues to share his dream, and I continue to listen, skeptically. "They are laughing quietly among themselves about something when they notice me and turn in my direction. I am actually there with them, and the feeling of welcome is like a friendly handshake. Then I speak, but it is really just thinking about how happy I am to see them; I don't really make any sound. They hear me, I know, and turn towards me, waiting. I ask the question I have for them, 'Is there life after death?' This proves I knew they were dead, because I knew they would know the answer! You get it?" Gene is delighted to share this conviction of his dream with me.

"They take some time to think about what I have said, look at each other. They are thinking it over, huddling up, like they weren't sure if it was all right to give this information out. Then Uncle Leon smiles the way he used to when he brought my mother chocolates, even though he knew damned well she was diabetic. You remember that look? Well, he smiles, shrugs, and they all turn to me. That's when the answer sails back to me like a boomerang: 'Look for pennies in strange places.' That was it, 'Look for pennies in strange places.' Then they all started walking away from me slowly, looking back, and smiling. My dad waves a little. I wonder where they were going, and why it was all right to leave me there. I felt, suddenly, like I didn't belong in their company."

The bedroom falls quiet for a few minutes as Gene recalls, and I analyze his dream message. It certainly was obscure enough to be a dream, and the message had a strangely familiar ring to it. Gene continues,"No matter what you say, you know I could never come up with a story like that unless it had really happened." He is waiting for me to discredit his experience in the interest of maintaining my patronizing position.

"It's fading fast, but I'm sure I was there, or they were here. 'Look for pennies in strange places.' What's it all about?" he turns to me for validation and explanation.

I begin by settling the pillows behind my head to augment the wake-up process. The familiar landscape of the field behind the Boemmels' house fills the windows I look from; the treetops are waving in the early morning light. In spite of the night visitors, I am in the familiar setting where I start each day of my life with Gene. I am happy and at ease with our predictable routine, changed on this day by his unusual dream.

"I think you really have had a pow-wow with your uncles and dad; I'll tell you why I think that. The message isn't as unconnected as you think. In fact, I have a chill running up my spine this minute. The answer they gave you, 'Look for pennies in strange places,' actually happened to me yesterday. Since I believe time doesn't work over there as it does here, that makes it more plausible. The fact is, this dream happened after my penny event yesterday, but that makes it more valid in my book and doesn't bother me at all. The boys knew you and I would eventually discover the shared experience of pennies in strange places. The question is, what does it mean, Genie?" I use the familiar term for him, first applied when he was a wonder man getting amazing things accomplished in another life earlier in the lumber industry. I take a moment to collect my thoughts. Gene waits anxiously to hear my interpretation.

"Yesterday, I was driving Eben to his drum lesson in a pouring rain. We were late getting started. I was rushing from one errand to another all the way to Saco. We decided to get a quick lunch at McDonald's in Biddeford. It was still raining torrents when we parked. As I locked up and followed Eben into the restaurant, I noticed a penny on the bumper of the car. I kept thinking about that penny all through lunch, and it bothered me, though I really didn't understand at the time. But as I kept thinking about it, I suddenly got it. There was no way a penny could have stayed on that bumper through all the road travel we did that morning. We were on the turnpike at seventy miles per hour. We turned left and right at many different intersections; all of this on the famous potholed roads of Biddeford, Maine…and in a downpour! No law of physics could explain how a penny stayed on my bumper all that time…and then, when we returned to the car after lunch, the penny was gone. I looked for it everywhere—under the bumper and around the area—but it wasn't there. I don't know what happened to it, but I think it reappeared in our bedroom this morning. I'm sure that's the penny your father and his brothers were referring to. But what is its relationship with life after death? I guess we'll just have to trust the boys for now and keep our eyes open."

Time, unyielding on this morning in 1989, continues to advance. The sound of traffic from Route One magnifies; cars from homes in the neighborhood back out of their driveways as their drivers head for Saturday chores and pursuits. Gene and I hear cartoons begin in the TV room and know the children are "into" their ritual Saturday indulgence. It's a good day when no one in the household has to go to school. Perking coffee sends a warm aroma up the stairs from the sleeping kitchen. The dream talk ends. A few years down the road, when I am alone in this room, in this bed, I will finally understand that the story I tell today begins here and now, in the events of this night; be they dreams or not. For the time being, pennies, the ubiquitous currency of everyday life, stay in their places.

July 1st, 1994

I am alone in an overheated kitchen on a very hot day. It is not just any day; it is my fiftieth birthday. I feel roasted, and I mutter at the counter as I half-heartedly prepare fancy food to be featured at a celebration dinner scheduled for tonight. I grumble under my breath over the circumstances that led me to be doing one of the things I most dislike; something I have dubbed "The Search for Food." In our many years together, Gene and I have entertained extensively, and this process of *food as performance* has lost any appeal it once had. We have decided to celebrate my birthday—really, I decided—with a dinner party to include our best friends and family; the people with whom we have spent the last twenty-four years sharing life's triumphs and hardships.

My husband is an endlessly frugal man, one who allots each and every cent to be spent in a week to small, labeled glass jars that circumstance and/or desire better not mess with. With frugality in mind at all times, he has accepted the responsibility of doing all the kitchen work for this party. Retired in January from his career as educational administrator in the middle school, Gene turned to cooking with an eagerness to try something new. Yet here I am, on a ninety-degree day, alone in the kitchen, sweating it out, literally, as I turn half a century old.

Everything was going smoothly in the planning stage; invitations had been sent out, supplies were gathered, and cleaning for the event is in full swing when the terrible news arrives from

Marblehead. Gene's oldest and dearest friend, Freddie Wilson, the man who arrived in the world beside him at the old Mary Alley Hospital, has suffered a stroke and died. Freddie suffered his first stroke a few years ago, but aside from some occupational/housing difficulties, has been in reasonably stable health, remaining comfortably in his home, still in Marblehead. The blow to Gene is visible. The two men maintained a warm friendship though their paths in life were very different. Freddie stayed in Marblehead and ran a lucrative auto-body shop. Gene, propelled by a determined mother, went to prep school at St. John's in Danvers, Massachusetts, and subsequently earned a B.A. and a Master's Degree in History, and a Master's Degree in Education from the University of Maine. In his career as an educator, Gene would go on with his middle-school staff to earn the National Schools of Excellence Award. All of this from a boy one of his principals, known as Gumshoe Gains employed by the Marblehead public schools, once predicted "wouldn't go anywhere."

Freddie and Gene remained fast friends, no matter the distance between them in miles, or no matter their life experiences. Their friendship was exclusive of the changes time had brought, and they were never far from each other in their hearts. On this day, Gene traveled to Marblehead in order to express his sorrow with the familiar community of family and friends the boys had grown up with.

The funeral was scheduled for the very day of the birthday bash. Tragic as the death was for its own sake, it is a very difficult development for the celebration. We consider postponing the party, but it's really too late for that. We had made reservations at a bed and breakfast in Bar Harbor for July second through the fourth, so we couldn't move the event to another day. We decide to carry on our plans; the birthday girl would just have to muster all her reserves and prepare her own feast. Standing alone in the roasting kitchen, I struggle to "handle" my feelings as well as the myriad tasks ahead of me...including the insult of making my own birthday cake. I feel abandoned and misused by the universe.

"I'll get home as quickly as I can," Gene promises. "We could still hire a catering company if we can find one this late in the game." But knowing the expenses already planned for the upcoming weekend, I choose to stay the course in this do-it-yourself mode. The familiar frustration with myself for creating such labor-intensive plans bubbles up. This is not what I want for my birthday, the one to mark the fabled day of midlife. My family genes predict long life and remarkable health, but the events of this day don't lead me to speculate on how I will enjoy it. I am marooned, trying to do my best, compromised by the intense heat and the piles of cooking dishes littering my workspace.

The birthday cake is the next milestone in the mountain of preparations: it can only be one of two cakes loved by and served for our tribe; the pure-chocolate layer cake with chocolate frosting, or the blueberry cake with lemon-butter frosting. I select the blueberry cake, as it fits with the availability of fresh blueberries in Maine in July. I attempt to sculpt a decent cake with the lemon-butter frosting, only to have the top layer glide on melting butter off the stack and head for the floor. I grab it with my hands and reposition it on top of the bottom layer, but it lists off the opposite side, creating a replica of that famous Italian tower. Something in me snaps, and the immediate solution to this problem appears. In a grand, sweeping motion, the cake is airborne, and it lands in the waiting waste can with a resounding plop; the top bangs shut, and I sink to the floor in misery. I lose all hope.

Just at this point, the door opens. Gene stops in his tracks. Then he dares the chaos he sees and crosses the family room to me. The whole story is readable in just one glance. In spite of the clouds of frustration gathering around me, he begins to laugh, and then, in a direct challenge to my emerging demons, he roars. His laughter does not endear him to me, but he has always been my savior in the tough moments of my life, and I can see he's just what I need. I laugh with him. Still laughing, he sits beside me and holds my hand for a few moments, and then we get to work. Gene has a talent for making the impossible, possible; the hopeless, hopeful. With his earnest, organized spirit in charge, the party will go on, and the guests, as well as the birthday girl, will be pleased. I know I can count on him. The evening is in good hands, because Gene is home.

Later that night, as we wait for sleep to find us, he tells me about the events of this monumental day: the funeral for his lifelong friend and the celebration we have just ended. It is a too-full day for one man's heart.

"Seeing Freddie buried was unbelievable. One of the hardest moments was just after the interment. We were walking away from the grave, anxious to get out of the burning heat, when a bagpiper standing on a hill opposite the grave began playing 'Amazing Grace.' We all stopped in our tracks and turned back and listened. A little breeze picked up from somewhere and rocked the coffin, which was suspended over the grass and dirt. It affected everyone; tears began to flow. I feel like I let him down in the last years of his life, because I didn't visit much. Who could have seen this coming? It's too late now." He feels the remorse of his inattention to his friend keenly.

Too late, indeed! The huge energy invested in the activities of the day take their toll on us; we kiss goodnight and move on to sleep. The morning holds our trip to Bar Harbor, Gene's birthday gift to me. The sorrow of Freddie's death, the party, and the next day's events weave their way into our dreams, but there is another with us in the room this night. It is already dwelling with us, although we don't yet know it. This presence sits Shiva for Freddie and is waiting for Gene.

beneath the pleasant street
dark waters swirl.
below the footsteps
of Sunday afternoons
and quick school mornings,
far beneath the mounds of cold snow
and thirsty roots of trees-
under the fire-hearted homes
of friends
the river Styx roils

JULY 4TH, 1994

The weekend away is wonderful. Bar Harbor rustles with activity in the advancing summer heat. A land mass subsumed by cold, gray fog and snow much of the year, it takes a long time for heat to crawl up the Atlantic coast and hold on for awhile. The nights are still cool, but the days are pleasantly warm. The town shines with preparations for tourists: flowers, lovely landscapes, and quaint architecture make a natural backdrop for strolling along and stopping to enjoy any number of views and delights. Signs up and down the street depict lobsters, paired with the venerable blueberry: blueberry pie, blueberry ice-cream, blueberry coffee, blueberry muffins, and on and on. The two colors, red and blue, are dominant hues in all directions.

Gene and I rest and explore, dine well and often, hike and walk and shop. We spend all of our time and most of our vacation money, and then it is time to head down the coast and on home in Kennebunk. It is July 4th, and we are due to host a cookout for the family at six o'clock tonight. We pack up, sign out of the B&B on Silver Street, and search for a coffee shop to get the obligatory cup of joe for the road. Gene is a coffee aficionado. The ritual of obtaining coffee has become one of his passions and an important part of our life together.

It is a life-long obsession that I, his life-mate, have watched develop and deepen. The Styrofoam cup teetering on the dashboard of our car is standard equipment for our family. We have even to wait our holiday celebrations for the procurement of the brown stuff. On most Christmas Days, we would both rise when the children could not wait another millisecond to open their gifts; that would usually be sometime between four and five a.m. (There were nights they didn't sleep at all, but played cards outside of our bedroom door just audibly enough to keep us from sound sleep.) The tree would have to be lit before they rushed into the room. There was a standing rule that they had to find the Baby Jesus I had hidden somewhere nearby before they could survey the loot. Rebecca had usually reconnoitered all the packages and knew exactly what she was getting anyway.

Then, there was an hour or two of surprise and contentment with the presents before Gene would stand up, stretch, and announce that he might just go out and see if he could find a cup of coffee somewhere in town, even though he would be holding a cup of coffee as he made this suggestion. We always set coffee up to perk at a certain time, so he was not deprived. But he wanted like mad to belly up to a coffee somewhere at the end of a tough reconnaissance. Perhaps it was a holdover from his army days. It was one of the deep satisfactions that lived in his hunter-gatherer's heart. In his line of work, planted in one place for so much of the day, he was denied intrigue, so he created small escapes for himself like these.

On this summer day in Bar Harbor, I stand, a witness to the ritual proving the depth of his bond to coffee. He is always poised to hunt strategically for the prize whether out in the frozen hinterlands of a Christmas Day or in the hot sun of a summer vacation. It put me in mind of the day he broke into a stakeout being conducted by the chief of police in Wells, Maine, bringing the man a coffee out of the goodness of his heart. The chief reportedly rose up from the bush he was hiding behind, shouting, "Graves, how in the hell did you find me?"

We stop long enough to find his coffee as we leave Bar Harbor, and because of this distraction, we are witness to prophesy. Walking toward the car with our prize, we hear the rattle of drums and the shrill notes of a band warming up somewhere nearby. A Fourth of July parade is just beginning; the route they travel makes us prisoners for now and the near future. The street is blocked by police cruisers. Crowds swirl into the vacated space with the elation and relief that protected law-breaking always provides. Everyone has a smile on their face. We are trapped and might as well give into the pervasive spirit of the moment.

Red, blue, and white colors everything: crepe-paper decorated doll carriages; bikes ridden by children of all ages, zigzagging down the street, preceding trucks and rescue vehicles idling as they wait for their place in the parade. Baton-twirling majorettes lead the band from the local high school, which, in turn, introduces the august town members of the past and present, gliding by in open cars flanked by police cruisers. They wave to the countless faces on the edge of the route, brightening when they see someone they recognize, but smiling broadly for everyone. It is a Norman Rockwell tableau.

On a whim, I grab the camera and back away from Gene as he stands there in front of the coffee shop. I snap a fairly close shot of him in his dark-blue shirt and khakis, holding *the* cup dearly and looking right at me with his warm smile. He is so content and hopeful, standing on that sidewalk in the faithful sun of that moment. This is the last picture ever taken of him, and I have it still. He is framed and venerated in my home as the saint he was.

Years later, I drive to Bar Harbor in perfect loneliness to stand in the footprints he is making now. I feel his presence then, with me, and I dare to look into the face of the past. This is something we, the bereft, do, attempting to find any trace of our loved ones here on earth and hold onto it like it would bring them close to us in some small way. But on this day in 1994, I am lulled into the comfortable progress of forever unfolding before us, one moment at a time.

The parade passes. We stand by our van, taking in the various floats and groups, when a hush proceeds up the street like a drum roll along with a particular tableau. In an attempt to provide a remembrance for all those who have died in the endless fight for freedom, the American Legion has created a graveside representation and it moves, accompanied by deep silence, into view.

The display is constructed on a flatbed truck and includes a row of chairs standing on a green sward. The chairs are provided for seated mourners; one seat is conspicuously empty, this chair being for the parade-watcher to occupy themselves and take part. The chairs face a grave that has been simulated on the float. The synthetic, glistening grass stretches up to the opening and beyond. There are flowers piled high; they shudder in the motion of the truck. All eyes are focused on a coffin suspended above the opening; it rocks slightly in the motion of the parade.

I hear Gene take in a quick breath, and I turn to him. With his glance to me, he whispers how this scene takes him back to the burial he attended just three days ago: Freddie's coffin rocked in the same way.

Along with the mourners on the truck, seven soldiers from the various armed forces ride, staring fixedly at a point above and far beyond the coffin. At a command from the officer in charge, they lift their rifles to their shoulders and fire three rounds. The bullets ejected at each round fly from the scene onto the street; children dive for them like candy. As the scene rolls past us, a soldier blows a mournful taps and the whole town of Bar Harbor seems to settle into a sadness that is in the wind, but unrealized until now. The sound shatters the notion that we are a safe little sea town in a large, safe world.

Gene salutes the flag, and I put my hand on my heart. The energy has shifted like a dark cloud covering the sun. The parade ends on this note, and people drift away quietly.

The streets unravel as the crowds leave. We do not talk as we drive toward home. The shadow has found us and follows. There is very little time left, but I still do not understand the riddle that is being posed. This bugle will sound again soon.

the hidden moon
rises
this night
in your eyes.
you are with him already,
looking away from me. you
feel him put out
into the current,
the strong, swift, sure slide
of black water
tugs at the bark
and you are away from me
and here
and now
and you go
with no hesitation.

July 10th, 1994

It is a hot Sunday afternoon. We are in Portland for some shopping and a museum visit with my brother Ted. Gene and I arrive early at the Portland Museum of Art and sit outside, watching the summer tourists glide by on the bright sidewalks. There is talk of Gene's birthday, only three days away now, and what he will choose for his all-important birthday dinner. This is the great privilege of birthdays in our family: we get to order dinner. Gene chooses (no surprise here) a steak dinner with baked potatoes and a salad from the garden we are growing at a friend's house, next door to my mother's, on Cat Mousam Road. Our backyard garden on Pleasant Street has been squeezed out by the trees and their shade, so we moved over two streets.

Gene is the gardener. He is a good one, although he manages to get through the reading of a few newspapers while weeding. It's his escape. His gardens obey his unflagging love of order. Every now and then, I invade his space with my airy notions of gardening, scattering seeds and plants every which way inside his orderly rows, but the garden soon adjusts and straightens out again. Gene's sense of order prevails.

Besides the steak and salad, there is the cake, of course. It will be blueberry, with lemon-butter frosting. We will mark his fifty-sixth birthday, and though it doesn't rank up there with my mid-century event a few days ago, it is of great importance to all in the family. We plan to plaster his picture on the front door and celebrate as much as we can on a Wednesday, though we have to work some of the day.

The planning goes on. We talk about Eben, our nineteen-year-old son, who is beginning to explore being the vegan he will become in later years. He will, most likely, decline the feast, but would never miss the famous cake.

My brother Ted and my mother are a constant presence in our lives and at our table, as was my dad and Gene's parents, for that matter, before they passed away. These dear people provide a continuity that reaches back to the very beginning of our lives together; one that blessed us in so many ways; living with colorful characters being just one.

My mother, Memere, suffers a view of the world in which expression tolerates no restraint; what she says has been unleashed by her age, her profession as schoolteacher in a one-room schoolhouse when she began her career, and a certain arrogance that comes from simpler days when people were more uniform. The variety of attire and lifestyles of the modern world leave her breathless sometimes; but opinion-less, never. We have to ride shotgun on each side of her when she is in public, or one of these days, someone might be tempted to deck her for her candid analysis. When she gets *that look* in her eyes, we scan the crowds for anyone who might challenge her idea of decency, and that could be for many reasons: dress, size, or career. She so annoyed a priest with her loud, pithy observations of the churchgoers during mass on one occasion, he actually reprimanded her from the altar. Such folks need immediate rescue, so we turn her around and march her in the other direction. Providentially, her vision is failing, and we usually are able to rein her in. She will be an honored and colorful guest at Gene's celebratory dinner.

Our family is very inventive in marking milestones and actually goes out of its way to concoct them. The *Last Supper* is one of our inspired creations. When a member of the family is about to be more than fifty miles away for awhile—this might include going to college, a vacation trip, a conference for Gene or me, or even the children's departure for summer camp—we throw a *Last Supper.* They are milestone events in our family life. Though we joke about the tradition, it is one we love to take part in, and it is meant to be fun, really; but in a way, we are conscious that the separation of loved ones brings the possibility of intervening fate. We keep it light, though, and the departing person names the tune for dinner.

Another of our traditions is *First Pesto Night.* The ripening basil and its slow process to becoming a rich, scented green sauce is feted during this dinner, when the first pesto sauce is made from the very intensely flavored tops of the new plants. On one of our *First Pesto Nights*, the bowl of precious green was dropped on the kitchen floor and smashed in many pieces. Not knowing how to respond to the tragedy, we danced around the precious substance, thus instituting a family tradition of dancing for the new pesto each year… We sing a verse we spontaneously created for the occasion: "*Oh the Pesto's on the floor, oh the Pesto's on the floor, on the floor, on the floor; Oh the Pesto's on the floor…*"; sung to a tarantella cadence. This ritual was replayed every year in the kitchen on Pleasant Street.

For our summer birthdays, and we are all summer birthdays, we prefer a meal on the deck overlooking the garden, one lit by a moon of any sort, plus candles and lanterns. This inclination for dinner parties has encouraged Gene to indulge his quirky sense of humor. Often, Gene organizes his fireworks routine. He secretly buys and hoards forbidden fireworks of all varieties whenever he gets the chance. Just recently, we broke into one of the locked metal safe boxes he had left behind to find a disintegrating stash of fireworks from ten years ago.

On the afternoon of any scheduled event he can possibly manipulate, he slips away to set up his treasures, hidden somewhere on our small in-town lot. Later in the evening, sitting around during or after dinner, he disappears for a moment, perhaps to "get more wine," or "use the facilities"; sometimes he just disappears with no explanation. After many years of marriage, I have come to notice his absence and guess what is about to happen to unsuspecting and suspecting guests.

Shortly after he returns to the table, a loud blast-off sounds out on the lawn, and Gene leaps from his chair in mock surprise and alarm. Our guests express a concern, but those in the know only laugh and look toward the founder of the feast, now standing and peering in the direction of the display in fake horror. Then the joke would be revealed, and we would all enjoy the fireworks.

Soon enough, the phone rings, and I insist Gene take the call. Of course, it is a neighbor complaining about the disturbance, intent on blaming Eben, who is innocent of the crime. Then Gene has his greatest thrill, owning up to being the culprit. In some way, this is his avenue to balance in the overly professional life he leads. He really enjoys becoming a rebel in a controlled incident like this. The neighbors never know what to say when, with a dismissive laugh, he claims responsibility for the disturbance. He assures them all is well, and that it won't happen again; but they know it will. He feels no chagrin and accepts no reprimand.

Rebecca, our twenty-three-year-old daughter is at Middlebury College, where she earned her undergraduate degree. She is involved in a program for the summer, along with her husband-to-be, Ahmet Bayazitoglu. They are participating in an immersion program in their respective languages, German and French, and they have signed oaths to speak only their language of choice, and so they may not talk with each other without breaking rules. She is also working in the administration program for some of her expenses. She is not coming home for the birthday, but will definitely call her dad.

Rebecca and Gene went out to purchase her first car a few weeks ago, when she was home for Father's Day, and to celebrate the twenty-fifth wedding anniversary of her uncle John and aunt Monica Fraser. We are reminiscing as we wait in front of the art museum now about her last visit. She and her brother cooked a wonderful breakfast for Gene and prepared to serve it on the side porch, since it was a wonderfully warm June morning. Her dad, again taken by his nomadic coffee-hunt compulsion, had gone down to the main street to get a paper and a secret Styrofoam cup, even though he knew the breakfast was in full preparation. Another of the little rebellions he practiced was the dismissive attitude he had for deadlines in a life littered with them. Here he came now, up the street, preparing to explain his tardiness to the assembled breakfasters who were patiently waiting as the food got cold.

On this morning, he literally glowed. Part of the decorations for the anniversary celebration the evening before had been the strewing of the tables with glitter dust. Before long, everyone had gotten the dust in their hair, on their faces, and on their hands and clothing. The guests all went home to sleep, glittering as much from the wonderful time we all had as the glitter dust. As Gene climbed the steps of the porch, gleaming sheepishly, we all enjoyed a laugh at his expense. The dust had stayed with him, and he was sparkling. The Father's Day brunch proved to be a great time. Later that afternoon, Rebecca and Ahmet left Kennebunk, honking and waving out of the driveway to return to Middlebury. She called her love back to us as she went up the street. We thought we would all be together again soon.

At this moment, in our musings in front of the building, Ted arrives, full of Sunday enthusiasm, from the parking lot next to the building, and our day at the museum begins. Our hearts are light and happy this day; all is right with our world, and we are secure in our lives. We travel the cool, dim corridors and rooms of the fine-art collection for a while, then spend time in the gift shop. As we emerge out of the cool, heady space into the bright, hot afternoon, Ted and I are talking enthusiastically about what we have seen. Gene is quietly walking a little behind us. Though this is not the norm, I don't notice until we exit the building and prepare for our walk to lunch on Commercial Street, a brief jaunt toward Portland harbor.

We turn downhill toward the sparkling harbor pooling below us and begin to pick up some speed. It is almost four o'clock, and we're hungry. We want to eat in one of the cool restaurants lining the cobblestone streets of the Old Port before it gets much later in the day.

Gene stops walking. Anchored automatically by his move, we turn toward him and wait with a question. He tells us clearly that he doesn't feel like walking to the restaurant, but will go to get the car and meet us at the corner of Commercial and Pearl streets. A man who ran up a mountain in Bar Harbor a few days earlier doesn't feel like walking a few blocks downhill after a relaxing afternoon. A man who walked vigorously for forty-five minutes or more most days of his life doesn't feel like walking down those pleasant streets with his wife and brother-in-law. *Do I hear what he is saying? Do I take it in and understand its import? Why don't his words blaze with the signal they have in hindsight? How did I become so lulled by the seeming permanence of our days and experiences together that I don't hear the voice of account telling me, "Prepare, make note, there is change in the wind."* Those voices sing to us on the streets of Portland, a chant that all is not well, after all; but I am not listening.

Gene turns away from us and walks to the car. Ted and I wave gaily as he passes us on his drive down the hill. Time moves as we do.

July 13, 1994

The birthday dinner is proceeding. We sit around the table in the large dining room of the old house on Pleasant Street, as we have been doing for thirteen years now. It is almost six o'clock, and the chocolate-brown walls of the room glow in the setting sun coming directly in the front windows. It's another very warm day.

There are four of us at table: Ted, Memere, myself, and Gene. Eben is practicing for a gig somewhere as the percussionist with his band, Blenderhead, but comes to remember his dad with a gift and a hug. He does not intend to stay for dinner.

I go to the kitchen for something, and when I return, what I see is etched on my heart. Gene is wearing his gift from his son. It is a bright red, logo-enhanced Blenderhead T-shirt. Gene grabs his knife and fork, raises them to bracket the steak dinner in front of him, and smiles broadly, his dear, brown eyes twinkling with happiness. He says with a sincerity that is deep, "This is the happiest day of my life."

We applaud and rejoice in being here with him. We look to each other to share and savor the moment. This dear man keeps us all afloat with his love, unselfishness and boundless love, and we are glad for him and of him. We're glad to see him ring in his fifty-sixth year, happy and whole. Rebecca calls from Vermont and has a short conversation with her father. At its conclusion, I hear him say "I love you, I love you." He repeats it and holds the phone for a moment after the disconnection before he puts it down.

July 14th, 1994

This day starts dull and quiet; the weather is cloudy, warm, and humid. I wake in the big bed before the alarm rings and snuggle against Gene's back, something I often do at the beginning of the day. The warmth of his body relaxes me and comforts me. I fall back to sleep for a while. Later, we both stir and list the day's needs and prospects to each other. *It was Thursday. Do you remember, Gene?* We plan to drive to Middlebury tomorrow to pick Rebecca up and continue on a short, weekend hop to Malone, New York, where we will visit Vera, Gene's aunt. Vera was born retarded and has lived with the family in Malone all her life. Since Nanny Graves's death in 1991, we haven't seen any of the New York family; it is time to pay a visit.

Gene is plainly worried this morning. His professional growth with the commercial realty firm he signed on with in Kennebunk since his retirement in January has been very slow. Though he spends thousands of hours in cold calls and hundreds of miles in footwork, he has not yet made a sale. I watch his sincere and diligent toil for the company, hear the rising criticism from his boss and the group, and begin to fear for Gene's happiness. The uncertainty wears on him, and this morning seems particularly hard. He doesn't smile and chatter over breakfast; he doesn't carry over the happiness of his birthday dinner to this day. He is somber and quiet, and I sense his unease.

We both go to the gym in Saco for an early workout. Gene follows me up the turnpike as I race along, trying to keep up with some invisible deadline in my head. When he arrives at the gym, he is appalled with me and alarmed with my driving. "Cynthia, you need to drive a tank when you drive like that." He offers his opinion. I am surprised at his tone. He is not usually so curt.

We part after our workout and go our separate ways for the day. Along with some colleagues from my high school, I am taking part in a special summer program based in conceptual-curriculum development at the University of Southern Maine. It has proven interesting and useful, and the new ideas will enhance my classes next year. We arrange to meet at five o'clock and go out to dinner with my mother before our weekend away. She is widowed, and Gene has been her caretaker lately as he works in town.

The day passes. I arrive home around four o'clock. The sun is behind clouds, and the air is muggy. As I look back, I mark the darkness in our home for that time of day. It is, after all, only one day after the glowing birthday party of July 13. I go along, turning lights on.

Eben is working his summer job at Dunkin Donuts in Wells. The house seems so empty. With both children now in their own lives, the twelve rooms we live in are very big, much bigger this night than ever before. I pick up a book and settle on the bed to read until Gene returns from his office, just down the street in the Lafayette building.

He is later than usual, and it turns into a long wait. It is very quiet; there is no neighborhood noise or traffic. I am restless, go downstairs to open some wine, and to set out crackers and cheese. Finally, I hear the porch door close after him and peer around the corner of the kitchen to welcome him.

Before I say anything, I am struck by his dark mood. It shows in his face and body. He looks like he is in pain, and, in truth, has a headache. He asks for some aspirin and flops into a chair; he leans forward with his head in his hands.

This unsettles me. I walk over to sit with the man who is always there for all of us. In this moment, the roles feel uncharacteristically and clumsily reversed.

I ask how his day has been, and he answers with a long sigh. Very concerned now, I sit opposite him and ask what is the matter. In a subdued voice, Gene describes an event that has taken place between him and his supervisor. The supervisor had become quite angry with him and called him into his office for a dressing down. I express my concern that this man would treat someone as earnest as Gene in that manner, but he reminds me, as if it excuses unkind and insensitive behavior, that this is not education, but "business."

The problem apparently seems to be that Gene was about to show property to some customers who had not been thoroughly "qualified," translate to mean, "verified to have the funds available and required by the property being shown." The man in question had yelled at Gene, saying harshly, "You just don't get it, Graves! This is a waste of your time and ours." This one encounter brings into focus Gene's fears about not succeeding in real estate, therefore letting down his loved ones, just when he is trying to find a new life for himself out of the disappointment that his career in education had become.

As an educational administrator of many schools and years, Gene had a solid reputation for respectful behavior with his staff and students. And so, this treatment today falls especially hard on him. Throughout his life, as a man of fifty-six, or a boy in his youth, Gene was unable to tell anything but the whole and perfect truth ever. This virtue was difficult to live with in our family, but it could be a real barrier in business. There is always a fact better left out when talking to customers, or the tweaking of small details expected by most people. Uncompromising, Gene would always extend the courtesy of respect to everyone he dealt with. I see quite easily where the conflict comes from, but this doesn't help my husband feel better this night. I offer him a glass of wine, and he accepts. While we talk, Gene asks me what I would have done had I been faced with the same situation.

Responding without hesitation, I answer, "Kick him in the ass, fight for your self-respect, and walk on. You're the guy doing the work. Don't let him get the best of the situation by feeling bad about it." My response is inappropriate to the moment, and Gene tells me that I am not really much help. He leans back in the seat, removing himself from this topic. The conversation shifts to other matters, such as the trip tomorrow and picking my mother up. I see, though, that this event has deeply affected him, and he is wandering, lost in a fearful place.

We go to the Blue Moon Café on Route One, just north of Kennebunk Village. On the way, my mother and I chatter about the weekend and how she will spend her time. My brother Ted is living in West Kennebunk for the summer and will be with her while we are away. Since my father's death in 1988, we are careful to see that my mother is not alone much. Gene remains quiet and doesn't smile at all. He is still preoccupied with the scene in the office this afternoon.

We are seated and begin ordering. In retrospect, time begins to speed up. Gene orders a seafood dinner, and for the first time ever in our lives together, he orders a glass of red wine to accompany it. As he has always been strong in the defense of white wine with seafood, I cannot contain my question, and I ask if he is sure he really wants red wine. Uncharacteristically, he glares at me and then replies defiantly, "I can order red wine if I feel like it." I agree and sidestep any further discussion about it. It is a small thing, but one that surprises a partner and causes concern to rise. He retreats into himself again and makes no attempt to participate in the dinner conversation. We finish our time with Mother, take her home, say goodbye, and go on in our evening.

The next stop is Dunkin Donuts to give Eben some instructions and spending money for the weekend, as he is not coming with us. He has finished his second year as a Performance Music major at the University of Orono, his father's alma mater, and has decided, to his dad's dismay, to take a year off and pursue his music career with his band, Blenderhead, in the bigger venues of Boston and New York City. He has also purchased a Vespa and taken to riding it back and forth from Kennebunk to Wells and home again after work. I fear a pothole somewhere with his name on it, and I endlessly caution him about this late-night travel.

When we arrive at the parking lot, Gene throws open the driver's side door and makes a beeline for the entrance. I am hardly out of the car before he is in and at the counter. He never even turns to let me catch up. This unusual behavior is enough to stop me in my tracks. By the time I get into the shop, he has ordered a coffee from Eben and is chatting with him as if I wasn't even there. Attributing this behavior to the afternoon trauma, I stand and look at him in some confusion, but decide not to bring it up. Later, I will remember these events and know it had begun already.

The moment has arrived, my darling. I try, even as I write this, to put it away from me, but I cannot. The last moments of our everyday life together have ticked away and gone.

Emerging from the Shop and Save with a few provisions— frozen dinners and peanut butter meant for Eben—we approach our car. My husband is forever the assigned driver of the family. There has never been a need for the decision about who will drive; it is Gene. In a moment of unrecognized intuition, Gene tosses me the keys instead. I catch them and change my course to the car, now going to the driver's seat. In just that action, a minor correction in the template of our normal patterns, an undisguised caution of some kind, he saves my life as he has so many times before. So much is happening so fast, that when I look back, I am dumbfounded that I didn't see the signs so evident in retrospect.

this night
you are still dying,
I run to shield myself
from your departure
in the empty house.

We have lived on Pleasant Street long enough that the way home is automatic. The big old house is always lit like a beacon, waiting on top of the upward swing of the street, whether anyone is home or not. One of our neighbors once kidded us the he didn't need to turn on the lights in his house, because he could see fine from the glow of lights in ours. As I turn onto the street, Gene is talking to me about something. As hard as I try, I cannot remember what he was saying; it was simply a conversation about one of the trite matters that concerned us. In the middle of the next sentence, his words shift from recognizable syntax to gibberish.

At first, I think he is kidding with me and making up for the long period of quiet and distance he has been exhibiting this evening. But he continues, and fear starts to play around the edges of my heart. We are almost up the street when I truly become alarmed and ask him to stop. I tell him strongly that he is frightening me. I turn from my driving and look at him.

It is there on his face: the outward signs of the rupture taking place in his brain. His look is one of confusion and distress, and he slumps in the seat. The side of his dear face around his mouth is collapsing and pulling up into the recognizable signs of a stroke.

He is still talking, trying to make himself understood. His hands and body begin to shake, and he slowly slips from the seat toward the floor, held in place only by the seatbelt.

Fear and adrenaline both roar into my bloodstream as I rocket into the driveway of our home. Flinging open the door of the van, I rush to his side, talking to him, begging him to hold on until I can get help. Then, I leave him and run into the bright house. I fling the groceries I somehow have in my hands into the sink. In pure panic, I grab the phone and dial 911. A dispatcher navigates my confusion to obtain the information needed to find us. They promise to be there immediately.

Then I am back at his side. I begin to try getting him out of the seat. He is bound up against the back of the seat by the belt. I struggle lifting him, and then I lower him onto the driveway. We finally achieve a position with him leaning against the car. He is quiet now, looking directly at me, blinking rapidly. Though tears are falling, I stay as calm as I can and try to reassure him that help is on the way, and that everything will be all right.

> *in the sink, where I have thrown it,*
> *the weekend melts*
> *its frozen moisture pools*
> *and puddles*
> *drips down*
> *the deep drain*
> *in long echoing, drops*
> *like rain*

Waiting for the rescue unit, I talk constantly to Gene about how things will get better for him. I am holding his hands. His eyes are still blinking rapidly, but he is quiet and does not try to speak. I know he is conscious that something terrible has happened.

It seems like forever before the rescue van slides silently into our driveway and the doors fly open. The men approach him swiftly and quietly. I feel tremendous relief with their arrival. Surely someone will know what to do.

Another car slides into the driveway, braking hurriedly. The son of one of our best friends, Jon Archibald, has heard the dispatcher on the radio and come to help. He is a practiced EMT; I strive not to register the dark looks exchanged between him and the paramedics. Their very slow, serious attention confirms the gravity of this event. They do not race the clock to get Gene to help, but rather, slowly and carefully brace his neck and head. They tell me to head for Southern Maine Medical Center. This measured, restrained response alarms me more than a hurried and charged rescue would. The metal clicks of the gurney being opened sound out; Gene is lifted in, and the doors close.

Jolene Lemelin, my neighbor, comes out of the dark toward me as I stand there, watching the rescue unit sink down the street. I begin the unconscious wringing of hands. She tells me later that we both spoke about the obvious, that life had changed forever for me on this evening. Jon, our friend's son, offers to go to Wells and bring Eben to the hospital. I ask him to make sure he doesn't ride the Vespa to Kennebunk first. It is not wise to leave another precious soul to the winds of fate blowing around us this night.

I turn to the looming house, unsure of how to proceed. The first person I can think to call is Monica, my sister-in-law. She is a registered nurse, and though she has been away from the practice for a while, she is familiar with the physical reality behind what seems to be happening. The phone rings, and she answers. The story of the evening doesn't take long to tell. She listens attentively, with soft sounds of compassion. I need her strong support. I have sought it before, and she graciously offers it. She is a person of courage and calm; the one we all go to in emergencies. She will come over immediately, and my brother John will go to West Kennebunk and alert Ted. The wheels of our sorrow are in motion. We decide not to tell my mother until tomorrow; her advanced age and frailty cause us to err on the side of caution for her.

I wait for Monica to arrive and reflect on this unexpected reality; I look out to the street constantly. From this point in time on, Pleasant Street will always carry the memory of Gene, my constant companion and defender, helpless beside me as we travel up its familiar contours to home. My future is to do whatever I can to help the dear man I have had the honor of being married to for 24 years now, to recover his life to the greatest measure he is able. This is my new life. It is very, very quiet tonight.

Not knowing if John has been able to get to Ted yet, I place a call to his summer cottage in West Kennebunk. He answers sleepily, and I realize that the hour has gotten late. I talk, and he listens. I hear the deep pain and shock in his voice as he asks the few questions he needs answered. He and Gene have become great friends over the span of years stretching from our wedding to tonight. In some ways, he is responsible for the wedding going off at all, as he distracted Gene while my mother and I had disagreement upon disagreement about the reception details, almost right up to the rehearsal dinner. Ted assured Gene that he was not in for a life of contentious bickering between wife and mother-in-law, and he was right. We are all good friends, particularly Gene and Ted. They see the world in the same way, politically and ethically, and they spend hours in discussion of world events. Ted offers to go to the hospital immediately. I am so immensely grateful for the presence of these people in my life.

When Monica arrives, we strike out together on the dark road to Biddeford. It is a foreign territory this night; the hospital seems very far away. All my senses are registering with skewed accuracy. I am dizzy and remote. We talk about the details of the stroke on the way up. She tells me everything she knows about the medical implications of a stroke. On our arrival, we are told that Gene's personal physician, Jon Shill, has been called, and he will arrive any moment. Our little group of four perches on the edges of our chairs in the family waiting room. We sit in a shocked quiet, still unable to believe what is happening, and wanting so to do something to reverse this fate enveloping all of us.

Dr. Shill arrives, comes to us, and explains that Gene has suffered a very serious vascular event in the left-lower quadrant of his brain. It is life-threatening; he is very careful to make us aware of this. He also informs us that in the process of preparing Gene for imaging procedures in the X-ray lab, he was accidentally dropped from the gurney. This terrible fact shocks us into silence. We can only imagine what the result of this accident would be to a man in the process of major stroke. He waits to discuss this fact with us, but we are in such a state of shock that we remain quiet; except for the most superficial questions. We can't imagine anything worse. It is only years later, upon seeing the actual medical records of the events of that night that I know Gene sustained a fracture of the right clavicle and facial contusions from the fall. I am so determined to save my husband's life with my bare will that I do not allow myself to focus on Dr. Shill's warnings.

I ask and am allowed to see my husband after the X-rays have been completed. Monica comes in with me. His limbs are in constant, random motion as a result of the damage to his brain. His eyes are closed, and he is not responding to events around him. I talk to him, reassuring him I am there, and that we will do everything possible to get him through this. I don't know if he hears or understands me; the center controlling his speech is damaged, and he cannot speak. I hold his hand, trying to suppress the automatic movement. It frightens me to see him in this condition. When I ask the attendants what they can do for him, they have no answer.

When I return to the private waiting room we have been shown into, Eben is there. He knows from the others what has happened to his dad. Stunned, we hold each other. I feel his vulnerability quiver through his summer shirt. His face crumbles in sorrow as he sinks into the nearest chair. He asks to see his father. About to turn twenty in a few days, his youth is so evident tonight as he stands here in his sneakers and Dunkin Donuts uniform. Barely three hours ago, he and his Dad shared a coffee and said goodbye for a few days. Now, in the sterile hospital emergency room, sadness engulfs us. I decide somewhere deep inside me that Gene *has* to survive this; anything else is unendurable for those of us who love him. I decide that it is my job to pull him through and bring him home to a family that cannot bear to conceive of life without him.

The time has come to call Rebecca. I have the phone number for the main office of Middlebury College. I know I can get in touch with the campus police, and they will carry the message to her. I call, tell them my sad story, and ask them to get in touch with her friend, Ahmet, so he can deliver this terrible news. I do not want her alone when she learns of her dad's condition. This is a difficult assignment, where neither may speak anything but the languages they are studying, French and German.

In light of the awful circumstances, the program requirements are waived, and Ahmet sets out to Rebecca's room. He gives her the news and the number at the hospital while we wait to hear from her. The phone rings, and when I answer, I hear terror in her voice. Ahmet has not been definitive with the details, so she still doesn't know who the message of alarm concerns. Rebecca asks if it's her grandmother, the logical person to be in difficulty. I reply in the gentlest tone I can find: "No, darling, it's Daddy. He has had a stroke and is in serious condition. I am here with John and Ted, your brother and Monica; we all think you should come home."

Her voice dissolves in tears over the miles between us. "Could you possibly be mistaken, Mom?"

After a few moments of silence, she accepts my words, and she decides that she and Ahmet will start for home immediately. Later, I hear that, in her pain and despair, she backs into the car of her supervisor, doing some damage as they leave the parking lot of the Middlebury campus. In an act of magnanimous compassion, no one ever pressed any damages against Rebecca. I will be forever grateful to them for their sensitivity and kindnesses to my daughter, and to our family.

The night deepens as we sit there: eleven o'clock; midnight. I assure Ted and John that it is all right to leave, and that there is little that can be done save prayer. Monica and I stay. Somewhere in the progress of time, we are informed that Gene will be transferred to the Maine Medical Center in Portland. Physicians are waiting there to do some diagnostic imaging. We drive after the emergency transport and see him as well settled as possible. He is quiet now, as the random body response to the trauma has stopped, and he is not in any obvious pain. Exhausted, we are urged by the staff attending him to let them do what they can until morning and to go home and try to rest for the ordeal still ahead.

We wend our way to Kennebunk on the empty roads, back to the huge, empty house on Pleasant Street, the house to which Gene will never return. I fall into a fitful sleep; Rebecca and Ahmet arrive a few hours later and wake me up. It is now Friday morning, and we face the process of trying to understand what has happened. When they wake me, I come out of my sleep and into the fear and sadness that has become my life. Rebecca and Ahmet take a quick nap before we go up to Portland. When we arrive, we find Gene awake, but still unable to speak.

Buoyed by his alert presence, we hug and hold him as much as we can and begin to feel some hope. He is quiet and serious, trying to communicate with us by gestures. We play a sort of game for awhile, one that feels better to us than to him, I'm sure. We allow ourselves to get quite lighthearted. Colleagues and friends of ours stop by. The normalcy of the visit lulls us into relaxing. Soon, though, Gene gets tired, and we leave to let him sleep.

The doctor to whom the case has been given corners me in the hallway as we exit the room. As I think back from this distance, I'm sure I never really allowed what he said to penetrate my hope. He talked of the *tremendous* trauma to the brain that Gene had sustained, and he told me that the damage from the event had just begun. His brain is ruptured. The crux of the prognosis will be the swelling that is yet to come. I repeat the mantra inside myself that Gene will come home, and we will defeat this threat to our being together. Nothing else is truly possible.

I begin, instead, to plan for his homecoming. In the hours between visits, I work to configure a house that can receive my husband as an invalid. The weekend advances in a strangely normal way. We cook food and sit together, sleep and wake and wait. After more visits and family discussions, Ahmet and Rebecca decide that they have to return to Vermont and continue with their language programs. We are lulled into believing, perhaps by my insistence, that this is a phase in his recovery, a situation that Gene can and will recover from. I continue to visit and hope over the next day. Things remain the same until Sunday morning.

July 17th, 1994

The weather is hot and muggy. I sit, reading in a corner of the living room in Kennebunk. It is very early in the morning. I will go to the hospital in an hour or so to see Gene. Somewhere in me, I know the day will end badly, but I will not let the thought into my conscious mind. I am searching for something to hold onto; some words to help me interpret what is happening. I need to wait a little longer before the visit.

In the empty house, upstairs, Eben is sleeping. He will go to the hospital with me today, as he has gone with me in the past few days. The phone rings, and I am puzzled about who would call so early. I rise to answer it.

Gene's Portland doctor is on the other end; I feel a rush of fear. He begins the conversation with no banalities; tired of my denial. "Mrs. Graves, what do you want us to do for your husband if he experiences a state of non-response? Does he have a living will?"

"We both have a living will, but you can't be telling me he is in a coma." I am desperate to refocus the conversation.

"I'm afraid he is. There has been massive swelling to the ruptured area. His bodily functions are being affected at this point."

I don't wait to hear more. "I will be right there," I holler before I throw the phone receiver across the room and run upstairs to wake my son. Eben responds to my alarm quickly. I hurry from him into the bathroom to shower and prepare myself for the awful day ahead. As the warm water rushes over me, I let my tears flow, as well as prayers of entreaty. The water carries them both away.

It is in this moment, somewhere in the space of the shower stall, that all the rules of physics and reasonable expectation are broken. It is here that the dream of my husband's uncles and his father comes back to point to the events waiting in the future. It is here, in the house on Pleasant Street, that a miracle happens. Along with the water descending from the showerhead, something plummets past my head and lands on the shower floor with a resounding smack.

In my distraught state, I imagine that Rebecca somehow has left her razor behind, or Eben has left his, and it has toppled off something and is now underfoot. I reach down to pick up whatever it is. The only object I can find on the shower floor is a *penny*. At first, I don't make the connection. I stand there with the penny in my hand, wondering. I hold it close enough to read the date: 1994.

With an audible rush, the dream of all those years ago comes back to me in every detail. I feel the powerful connection between that dream and this penny. To me, it is a sign; a sign that someone is watching over us. *"Look for pennies in strange places. Look for pennies in strange places."* In some parallel time zone, those dear old men knew that we would have this agonizing experience, and they were weighing in, back then, with evidence of connection, hoping to offer direction to us through this terrible experience. I cling wildly to this idea, not allowing myself to plumb the actual meaning in this small coin that I hold.

I had allowed myself to forget the question posed in the dream. The question was, *"Is there life after death?"* In this guise, the penny is a resounding *"Yes,* there is life after death, and this you will have to trust soon." It is not long before the consequence of the message descends on me, and I have some sense of what waits for us in the next hours. Time is running out.

Somehow, Eben and I arrive at the medical center after the tense, quiet ride. We know all the way that Death is a passenger with us. It is hard to understand how everyone we see is so happy and busy with their lives while our hearts are breaking. The very air hangs, too heavy to breathe.

When we arrive at Gene's room, the door is closed, and we are barred from entry; he is receiving emergency procedures. When the door opens, a very serious group of doctors and nurses leave in silence. Soon enough, we are informed that they have been attending him in a choking incident. His body is beginning to fail, and he is still in a non-responsive condition. They let us into the room, and we are stunned to see him in this state. This man who was the answer man in times of doubt and confusion; the comforter for all of us in times of difficulty rests here in trouble himself and we don't know how to save him. We hold his hand, stroke his very submissive body, and call to him, but he does not respond in any way at all.

Eben goes out to the hall for a moment. The reality of what is happening suddenly emerges clearly and moves me to action. I circle to the right side of Gene's head, knowing that the trauma in his brain has left him deaf in his left ear, though he is able to hear in his right. I take his hand in mine and begin to speak to him as the person I know and love. There is no time for pretense; I am direct and calm. My tears are flowing again, but this has become usual. I don't swerve in my purpose. "Darling, I want you to come home. I am preparing everything for you. I will be there, sweetheart, don't worry about anything. I will redo your office for a bedroom for as long as you need it." Then, though it is the hardest thing I have ever said, some angel leads me to go on with my farewell, in spite of how terrified I am in this moment. I speak the words that allow the unimaginable into the room:

"If you can't come home, Gene, darling, if we have to part…" The words come hard, and sobs separate them. "…if you can't come home to us, I will do everything I can to take care of the children and give them what we wanted for them. I will take care of myself, too. I love you, and I can't bear being without you. Please hear me and come home." I realize that Gene is squeezing my hand now, strongly, over and over. With firm pressure, he answers me, hard and sure; and then, he just stops.

> *and the ferryman*
> *poles his passenger*
> *to the river Styx,*
> *endlessly quiet now,*
> *onto that other river,*
> *Lethe,*
> *its waters reflecting*
> *the sky in perfect circle,*
> *seamless and serene*

Eben returns to the room and takes his father's other hand. We stand that way for a few moments, then the nurses ask us to leave. Gene's physical state is in freefall now; they need to suction fluid from his lungs. For an eternity, we stand in the hall, as caregivers come and go in hurried concern. Finally, they tell us it will be hours before we can see him again. We take our hearts in our hands and return silently to our car. We drive home, confused and afraid of the obvious course of the events of the day. We call Rebecca, advise her that she should be prepared for anything, and that she should return home.

The day is still Sunday. A neighbor sends over a casserole and family members drift in, grimly aware of the prospects for Gene's survival. We all sit around the table, trying to understand what has happened. We just don't know what to do.

Weston Graves, Gene's Marblehead cousin calls, gets directions and goes to Portland to be by his cousin's side. On his was back to Massachusetts, he stops at the Pleasant Street house to share with us what he has seen and what he thinks. We are just leaving for the hospital when he arrives. He suggests softly that we have Gene transferred from Portland to Biddeford so he is closer to home. I'm sure he has seen that there isn't much time left, and no treatment will reverse the damage already sustained.

To us, in our denial, it feels like some action we can take to be closer to our loved one, and his trusted friend and physician, Dr. Shill, would regain charge of his case. Arrangements are made easily, and the move is initiated. The staff in Portland has done all they can.

My brother Ted accompanies me to the Southern Maine Medical Center to be present when Gene arrives. We enter the room, hopeful to see some of our dear heart's presence. We see instead that Gene is in a deep coma; unreachable. We sit with him, now unable to deny what is plainly before us. The comfortable space between tragedy and our personal lives disappears; they are now the same thing. We sit for a long, silent time.

Dr. Shill arrives and does a cursory examination. He tells us that the coma is advancing. There are no positive signs here. He cautions that we must not read any hope from the deceptive peace Gene seems to be in. This coma is the mark of his swelling brain. He advises me that this will be a long night and will probably end badly. I should go home and get any rest I can, and he will call me if he needs to. With a kiss on the forehead, I leave this man who is my heart. I will not see him again in any earthly form.

JULY 18TH

We are at home. It is morning. The house is still deep in silence and rides on the street like a ship in fog. Every familiar landmark is gone. Only Eben and I are there. During the long night now behind us, the phone beside my bed has rung every few hours, shocking me out of the lethargic daze I have descended into. Relentlessly, Dr. Shill checks in with the details of Gene's departure; his brain has continued to swell; his organs, responding to the trauma, shut down; he is placed on life support. He is still in the cruel coma that I last saw him in. I listen and pray…I do not go to the hospital. This is something that I find hard to explain to this day. I do not leave my bedroom and go to his side. I know that nothing can stop the journey he has begun, and I cannot watch with him.

We have placed a call to Rebecca and Ahmet, telling them that they need to return. In an attempt to keep her father safe in her mind, she tries to deny the seriousness of our voices, but cannot. The painful truth has been unleashed in our midst. When she arrives somewhere around seven in the morning, we all prepare for the meeting Dr. Shill has requested. The somber family members gather at the house on Pleasant Street. I am so grateful to have them around us; their support sustains me. They are sorry and gentle; it breaks my heart to be the portal through which such pain enters their lives. Ted, John, and Monica come out of love for Gene and sympathy for Rebecca, Eben, and me. None of us has ever experienced this level of sorrow, and we find that we don't know how to go forward.

At eighty-six years of age, my mother stays at home on Cat Mousam Road, rosary beads in hand, praying for the best for all of us. She wishes to be left out of the actual events, as her physical state is fragile. She is a person of great faith, and though none of us can even think to pray, she takes up this duty willingly.

We drink endless cups of coffee, trying to think around what is to be done when there are so few options. Finally, we leave for our meeting with Dr. Shill at the Medical Group offices. He describes Gene's condition and diagnosis in clear terms, all the while, bearing a sympathetic demeanor. Gene is being kept alive by artificial means and has no chance of survival on his own. He would succumb to death if taken off the equipment. Dr. Shill knows of Gene's living will, and suggests that we comply with his wishes, as impossible as that action may appear.

An enormous silence hangs in the small room when he is finished. It presses on all of us with its weight. Time slows way down for me. I am dizzy and disoriented.

The action is mine to take. Everyone defers to me, and I am paralyzed. I ask the simple question that is at the core of this awful moment. "*Is there any hope—no matter how remote or faint— that Gene would be able to claw his way back to us?*" Knowing Gene as intimately as I have had the privilege, I understood his commitment to us is embedded in the very fiber of his being. He is the man who, to make us laugh on difficult days, would open the driver's side door of his car and fall out in traffic at stop signs, no matter what other travelers thought, just to bring a smile to our faces. This is the man who, when I was depressed because we had moved away from Kennebunk to facilitate a career opportunity for Gene, crouched beneath our new bedroom window and made the sounds of a neighbor babbling while he worked in his yard, hoping to make me feel like I was "at home." This was a man who loved us to distraction. *Could he overcome these physical barriers and come back to us?* Somewhere in me, I still hoped he could come home.

Dr. Shill is clear, emphatic, and sincere in his response. There is no basis for hope of Gene's regaining any consciousness. In fact, his liver and kidneys have shut down, and there can be no reversal. The decision to remove him from life support is the only one that allows my husband the dignity of a merciful death.

Knowing I will have to live with the outcome for the rest of my life, I ask again: "*Can Gene possibly outlast this physical trauma and return to consciousness, even if it meant he would be an invalid and have to depend on others to keep him alive?*" I assure Dr. Shill that I am ready to assume that duty and would do anything to have him home again. I press him, realizing I am only a few words away from the most horrible thing that could happen: a separation from my beloved husband. His word will have to be my guide.

He realizes the import of his reply, and he takes a few minutes to think the situation through one more time. He looks around to all the gathered family and then restates his answer gently, but firmly, in the most emphatic terms he can: "*There is no way back to life. Gene is waiting to be released.*" He looks at me and tells me to be ready for terrible times ahead.

The plans are made. My brother Ted agrees to meet Dr. Shill at the hospital this evening at eight o'clock. He will be joined by Gary Archibald. They will stay with Gene as the support is disconnected and will wish him well into his new life. Dr. Shill will administer morphine if there is any discomfort. He is very insistent that he be there, as Gene was a friend of his and long-time patient.

I see everything swirl past my affect. I can control nothing. Dr. Shill offers me a tranquilizer, and I accept. I decline to be present at the hospital as Gene dies. I know that this scene would replay in my heart for the rest of my life; I can not endure the moment or allow this image into my life. This decision will give me much conflict in the future years, although I know that Gene would have forgiven me. He often talked, during our lives together, about his wish not to be exposed after his death and we will honor this wish. There will be friends by his side when he departs this earth, Gary Archibald, his colleague and companion, my brother, Ted, who will honor their friendship, and Doctor Shill himself. These plans made, we leave, heavy-hearted, and go back to Pleasant Street.

There descends a protective curtain between ourselves and terrible events like the one we are all facing this day. Almost surreptitiously, life moves us on, ready or not, and I must go on, too; at least in time, if not in mind. Once back at home, I begin to clean with a vengeance. The old ark of a house that has shielded our family for many years now becomes an industry of refuge. I am conscious of the public ceremony about to play out within these walls. It saves me from confronting what is beneath the tide of hours that comprise the day my husband will die.

I concentrate on clutter and dust. Dirt on the floors becomes my enemy and my ally. The thirty-five windows get polished; the laundry that has piled up during the last days gets done; I do not, cannot stop. What my dear children think and feel is far from my awareness, for I can't save them from this anymore than I can save myself. We begin conversations and drift away from them in the middle of sentences. I retreat to scrubbing and arranging and rearranging. I take refuge in worry about the grass, the deck, the food for the funeral; about anything. These things are still under my hand. Gene is leaving us.

Food, once the raison d'etre of my role in the family after my mother, also disappears from my radar screen. I don't eat or cook anything. Mealtimes come and go. Where they were once the measurement of time, now time is unfettered and sifts with the hot, July breeze. I nap in the afternoon and remember only the darkening of the light as I awake. I am afraid of this darkness; afraid to see the sun fall in this evening. Somewhere in some deep channel of consciousness, I feel I need to begin the requiem that will attend the events of tonight. It is, in fact, a holy night, and it needs to be marked.

I begin to search out all the wonderful moments of our twenty-four years together. I open drawers and photo albums, look in shoeboxes stuffed with prints from all the years, and compile a life study from these once unimportant photos: pictures of the newlyweds in front of their first home, happy and hopeful; pictures with our friends and family, mirroring back a life full of love and fun; the newlyweds in front of their first house, by a campfire on the cliffs overlooking the sea; skiing at Sunday River; parties and dinner around the well-known dinner table in all of our homes; in our gardens in West Kennebunk; on Pleasant Street; on the trips we took as a family to Prince Edward Island; to Paris; to Sturbridge; pictures of the fantastic faces of our children who are still the greatest wonders on the face of the earth to us; pictures of birthday parties, with the cakes down through the years; and of Christmas Eve gatherings at my mother's house or at ours. In one, we are still singing, the four of us, open-mouthed and cherubic, in such a time of peace and joy. High school days of Rebecca and Eben live again; soccer and plays and all the precious faces of the friends our children brought into our home, the leave-taking for college, at once glorious and tragic...in all of these vignettes of our lives, Gene is gracing us all with his love and care. I lay these miracles of love and life and friends all over the house, make little altars on which I light candles as the light dims on this day, July 18, 1994, the day Gene must die.

From somewhere, people begin to drift into the house, without any invitations, they just come. Word has gone out in our circle: Gene is leaving all that is known to us; going with those who have gone before. This is a departure to mark with reverence and sadness, but also it is cause for gratitude for his time among us.

We all sit in the dusk, in the candlelit dusk. Rebecca and Eben are here with their friends, in their own world of grief. Their friends are stunned with disbelief that this could really happen to one of us, one of the people in this little world of Kennebunk. It has always been such a safe life we led. There is soft talking, and coffee brews. We all await the return of the watchers.

I lose myself for a moment, telling the story of how Gene and I met. It is a wonderful tale. I was working for the summer teaching theater for an Upward Bound program. It had been a tumultuous summer, full of deadlines and challenges, and I was ready for change and rest. Our staff had been trained by Outward Bound program instructors, a survival-type group process. We were not told what to expect when we got off the boat on Hurricane Island. As a naïve girl from Rumford, Maine, I had prepared myself for the experience by packing a cocktail dress, my hairdryer and a carton of cigarettes, not exactly the equipment most people expected the participants to arrive carrying. This set me up for notoriety, as no one had ever brought a cocktail dress to the island before, and I quickly became a poster girl for the "before" segment of their training program. I received special treatment for this from the beginning.

Not appreciating their attitude, I challenged the staff of the program as to their definitions of "success" and refused to participate in many of the activities of the week. Consequently, things did not go well.

We were asked to run every morning and leap off the dock into the cold, June sea. I could hardly breathe at that time, because of my smoking habit. Another of the tests of strength and courage involved rappelling from a steep cliff wearing a safety harness. The rappel coach was more interested in my phone number than in giving me instructions to step off that cliff. Needless to say, I made history, but that is another story.

This experience, along with difficult teaching duties over two months, left me exhausted, anxious to finish the program, and looking forward to Wells Beach, where my parents rented summer property, and we all gathered for the month of August.

Gene and I had taught together the year before at Mexico High School, in Mexico, Maine. We had spent some time together as friends, but had not dated; in fact, he was engaged earlier in the school year to a teacher with the same last name, Fraser. That relationship had broken up, but being the very shy person he was, he had not made any attempts to date anyone else, though many of his colleagues would have been glad to oblige.

Gene was working as a summer policeman in Wells Beach to augment the meager salary of a teacher; he had somehow learned my parents were in Wells, and that I would spend some time there in August. During my time teaching in Gorham State College, as it was known then, he called and asked me to go to a play with him at the Ogunquit Summer Theater. I accepted and looked forward to spending time with him, as he was an interesting and quite attractive friend. On my way to my parent's cottage in Wells at the close of the program, in my state of exhaustion, I nearly had a very serious accident. I woke up suddenly on the other side of the white line after drifting off to sleep and almost didn't recover control of my car. I only avoided another car by a miracle. This alarming event, coupled with being twenty-five and unattached, with very little direction in my life, left me feeling vulnerable just as I drove into range of Gene Graves.

The date had been set for the evening of my arrival, but for some reason, I didn't know exactly the time he would pick me up. After I rested and recovered a little from my drive, I got dolled up and went out to find my date. I jumped into my Camaro Super Sport convertible and searched the small town over for a police car or an officer with his friendly smile.

It had been raining, and the sky over Wells was dark and gray that afternoon. As I approached the center of the town, the traffic was snarled, and down the road, someone was in the street, directing cars out of the impasse. I parked my car and started towards the officer, thinking it might be Gene. Just as I came up the street to the crossroads, the clouds broke, and a shaft of sun the color of liquid gold shot out and illuminated the officer at the center of the road. It was Gene all right, standing there in the middle of it all, backlit by the gray clouds, but glowing in the sun, directing traffic as if he had been doing it all his life.

He saw me, broke into a lovely smile, and called out, "I'll pick you up for dinner at six…I know where your parents are renting. Glad to see you." Then he went back to work, and I just stood in wonder at the scene before me. This golden boy charmed me with his magic in that very second, and, in the weeks to come, he offered me the pleasure of a intelligent, warm, sincere friendship. I went back to my car slowly, a warm feeling bubbling up from my heart. We never were apart again.

But I have gotten lost in the telling of the tale. The room is silent. Looking around, I see that the faces turned to mine are full of compassion and sadness. For a moment, I wonder why. Then, I remember.

This is the way the parting takes hold: in steps descending to, facing the enormity of what is happening, and then retreating from the powerful pain of this present. No one can stand the experience of such potent pain for long. There is an automatic protective response that leads us away from the truth and into a palpable experience of happier days.

They come. The car swims up the street in the thick dusk, its lights carving a path before it, and slides into the driveway. The watchers approach the house, and I know that my husband is dead. The silver cord, slim as it was, is cut. He is free of the weight; the fear and the pain of the human state. But, what, oh God, will we do without him?

JULY 19TH, 1994:

THE ARRANGEMENTS

Consciousness returns me to a new world the next morning. The first thing I see is the portrait of Gene on the night table beside me. As I allow the knowledge of his death to surface, the picture seems to move. The energy of my dear one is trapped behind the glass of the frame and I pick it up, holding to my heart. Tears flow; they have become the currency of the realm. The face I know so well draws me to it, and I talk with him in sad wonder of the events that have separated us physically. It seems to me that he is somehow "in" the photo I hold. I am almost sure he is responding to me as I speak to him.

There is a minefield of his belongings to negotiate while dressing; his bathrobe, still scented with the cologne he loved to overuse; the pile of books he left unread on his night table, one open and face down as he left it; his shoes…oh, his shoes: polished and lined up to carry him onward in a life that has secretly completed. I spend the morning touching every sacred thing that once connected him to this place and to me. As the keeper of the memories, I know every minute detail about this man and our life together; I will forget nothing, ever.

When I arrive in the kitchen downstairs, there are people I don't recognize right away. A few friends and neighbors are here, but they seem like strangers on this day. They are anxious to help, but I can't think of anything to do. The children wait for me to act. Oh, God, it is Eben's birthday; he is twenty years old today. We begin to talk about how to proceed. The work of preparations and schedules lies before us now, the public ceremony must be performed, and it must be worthy of Gene. As things fall into their proper priorities, the birthday will have to wait.

Someone calls from Bibber's Funeral Home to inform me gently that Gene's body has arrived. Gene, who cannot pick up a phone and call or come home, again, is waiting silently in a dark room in that stately gray establishment. My brother Ted arrives and suggests that we all go to the funeral home to make the arrangements. In a moment of escape, I remember Gene could never say "funeral." He always slipped into a childhood pattern and said "fruneal." I'm the keeper of that memory, too; of every detail of our lives still present just behind the scrim of every day. It will be many years before the sun will rise on a day that lives in the present.

Dick Bibber, a fellow Rotarian and a friend to Gene, meets us respectfully at the door. Dick is famous for gliding around Kennebunk in his black limousine, his finger pointing ominously as if he were the Grim Reaper himself. This was his way of waving to his friends in town. Gene would often be the object of the finger as Dick passed us on our daily walk that took place in all weathers. We laughed at the joke then. Today, the demeanor of Dick's greeting is solemn.

It is very hot and humid. The magnificent old trees around the gray Victorian house sway in a swirling breeze. They seem to be brushing up against me in consolation. The details of the "fruneal" are easy; they spin themselves out of all the discussions Gene and I have had about the celebration of passing onto the other world. I know all the answers to the question of what Gene would wish. The casket will be closed; we will do a photo display. There will be a funeral mass at St. Joseph's Church, in Biddeford, at noon on Thursday, the twenty-first of July. Burial will be in Hope Cemetery in Gene's beloved Kennebunk, beside his mother and father, who have died before him. My husband always said he wanted to be carried out of our home on Pleasant Street feet first. As he wished, that had happened.

In a special direction articulated by my husband when speaking casually about his funeral, he wanted whiskey rings left on his coffin from a final toast. Accordingly, we will invite his close friends to stay behind after the wake concludes and drink to Gene. They will be asked to raise their glasses to his memory and slosh some whiskey on the casket, leaving their glasses behind as a testimony to this man and the fulfillment of his wish.

Dick Bibber reminds me that Gene's body is in the next room, just a breath away. He asks if I want to go in and spend a few moments with him; he knows that closure for the bereaved often depends on seeing the reality of death on the loved one. I appreciate his concern and expertise, but I cannot go in. The fear rising in me is big. Today, after the ensuing eleven years of working myself into accepting the reality, I could do this; but on this awful day, I shake my head and the children do, as well. We are too deep in denial and shock to see this man of ours so still. I ask instead that Dick get the wedding band Gene wears, one of a matched set we had made when we were engaged in 1969.

He is gone for just a moment. I am stunned by the evident nearness of this man of my heart. When Dick returns, he hands me Gene's ring. I notice that it is cold. I put it on and know that I will wear it for the rest of my life. It warms on my hand quickly; I feel connected to Gene in this vow.

Over the years, I have suffered for not seeing my husband out of the world. I fear that he felt abandoned or afraid. We had many discussions about life after death, and his position was that viewing of the dead was neither endurable nor desirable. He always strove to keep the person alive in his memory, and though he attended wakes in respect, he didn't like the ritual. We keep that in our hearts in closing his casket. I hope he forgives me my fears. We have a video of Gene on the night of his retirement party, December, 1993. Though I keep it as a sacred remembrance, I have not watched it. He promised me often that if he died before I did, he would, if he could, come back to tell me about it. It was not long before he kept that promise.

July 19th, 1994:

The Preparations

Later that day:

But now, there are things to do, and we throw ourselves into them. Rebecca, Eben, Ahmet, and I go to Portsmouth to buy funeral attire. There is a moment in downtown Portsmouth when the little group disperses to individual stores for various reasons. I am left standing on the hot sidewalk, alone. I see myself in the windows I walk past. I have no reference point left at all. I don't know how old I am, where I am going, or who I seem to be. All those certainties are gaping holes in my present. My reflected image is one-dimensional; I fill it perfectly in this moment.

The heat keeps up, and we stumble into an Indian restaurant for lunch. We order numbly and sit, making whatever conversation we can in this new world. We order wine and lift our glasses to Eben on his birthday. There will be no cake today. The familiar birthday ceremony or cake is inconceivable in this island of time.

July 20th, 1994

The Wake

The wake is a social success. The number and commitment of those who attend is gratifying. Though difficult to understand, the paying of respects to Gene and his life dulls our pain and diverts our attention, for the immediate time. Sandra Harvey, a colleague from Gene's years at the middle school in Kennebunk, is the first person through the door. Strangely, Gene had been concerned of late that she was angry with him for some reason, and he worried obsessively about this as he passed her house on our walks. I want to tell him that he was wrong, but it is too late. Gene is no longer there to tell; just Sandra with me in this terrible ordeal.

The Masons arrive in their feathered attire, swords clinking. Gene and his father were members in Marblehead, though they did not attend meetings. In spite of this, they perform their extravagant funeral ritual in proper formation. As they point their fingers abruptly upward, they remind us all of our final destination. I am thankful for their loyalty to Gene, a Mason who never attended a Masonic meeting in Kennebunk for the nearly thirty-five years he lived here. They pass the Catholics, who are entering as they exit.

Gene was a convert to the faith early in our marriage. I impressed on him that it was not necessary to make the switch for me. He persevered and came to really love the mass and scripture.

I feel buoyed as the rosary starts and our wonderful community of friends from St. Josephs gathers round. A man of great humor, Gene would enjoy the juxtaposition of these two religiously exclusive camps meeting at his wake.

The two sessions at Bibber's pass in a flash. We are astonished and affirmed by the outpouring of support and love we receive. Students from Gene's teaching days, students he helped in so many ways, parents and colleagues, our friends and social acquaintances; so many people that I feel giddy in the influence of their love and concern. As the last minutes tick by, the door is closed to the public, and a few personal friends stay behind to enact the requested ceremony. Dick Bibber retrieves the bottle purchased for the event and pours drinks all around. We lift our glasses in a final salute and drink. The bitter whiskey is a fine marker for this bittersweet moment, and the warmth slides into all of us. We leave our glasses on the casket, turn our backs, and walk back to our lives.

THURSDAY, JULY 21ST

THE BURIAL

It has been one week since the last ride with my dear Gene, up Pleasant Street. It is his funeral day. If I had cleaned before to escape the reality accumulating at my feet, I begin now to clean for my life: the house, the deck, the lawn, just about anything. On the morning of the ceremony, I rise to cut the grass at 7:30. Rebecca leans out of her window and waves for my attention. I have disrupted her sleep; sleep she has had precious little of lately: *Could I please wait until nine o'clock?* she asks gently. I realize I have no notion of what time it is, but I am afraid to turn off the lawnmower and go back into the too-quiet house. Through sheer power of will, I manage to turn it off and slip into the house to arrange and rearrange anything I can find that looks the least bit asymmetrical. I am unstoppable in my fever of grief.

Soon enough, the black limousine slides up the street, and we embark on the voyage that will end in Hope Cemetery this afternoon. Gene will take his place with the departed townsmen and women of Kennebunk; this will please him, I know. He loved Kennebunk, and he invested this town with a notion of pristine quality; he saw democracy and high-mindedness at work in the lives of the common people. I was not so easily convinced.

The temperature soars; the sun is out in full throttle. Again, I think how Gene would have loved the weather allotted for his funeral.

We leave Kennebunk, following the hearse, and travel to Biddeford in our sad convoy. It is Thursday; we pass the Glenmore Restaurant. The Rotarian sign proclaiming the location as the meeting place on Thursdays at noon reminds me of the call I had from the current president of the group. He asked if I realize that I have chosen the exact meeting time of the club for Gene's funeral. This presents a conflict to the group as to whether to attend their meeting or go to the funeral of a loyal member.

I reply that, no, I didn't realize that my choice of funeral schedule made it difficult for the members. I don't explain that the Rotary Club hasn't been in my mind for one single, solitary heartbeat in the last week of despair. He seems apologetic. I sound as stunned as I am with a petty complaint and implied disapproval. This only confirms the longstanding joke between Gene and me that I made a lousy Rotary Jane; the sort that resented the pies I had to bake for "Rubber Chicken Night," the euphemism for the Rotary Cookout. I resented being marginalized in the role of the dutiful wife, and was often loudly vocal about seeing the usual hierarchy of self-important leaders evolve, to the detriment of this group. The absence of sincerity of feeling for one of their devoted, if unappreciated, members adds credence to my suspicions. But I don't say anything about this. My mind and heart are elsewhere.

When we arrive in front of the old brick cathedral of St. Josephs in Biddeford, the temperature on a sign we pass registers ninety degrees. The bell in the tower starts to toll, its sweet tones pouring down upon us as we alight from the car like rain. In front of the church, a crowd waits. I see faces I haven't seen for many years. My heart contracts in response to the obvious care they have for us and our tragedy. For a moment, I forget why I am here. I rush to greet people from all eras of my life: high school friends, colleagues, and family friends from Marblehead and Rumford offer me a hand and a hug, holding me on this sidewalk; holding me still just now. I am so still, but Gene is still forever.

At the door of the church, Father Mark waits for the body to be lifted up the stairs to the vestibule. The hot wind helps lift the coffin, which is attended to by a coterie of loyal, sweet faces. My brother John is there, as is Gary Archibald and Jon, his son. My closest colleague, Dan Joseph, also a friend of Gene's, and Chad McDonald, my son's good friend in high school, along with Ahmet Bayazitoglu, my daughter's husband in the future, take the terrible weight of this journey. Rebecca, Eben, and I take our place behind the casket, and we begin the long journey down the aisle. We hold hands and walk, looking straight ahead. There has been little concern with our appearance; tears flood down our tired and drawn faces. We sit in the first pew, watching and listening, as if in a trance. Behind us, my brothers and Monica sit. Behind them, ranks of others send us support. I feel their energy at our backs. I could not survive this loss without them.

The liturgy of the mass begins to unfold on the altar, familiar and comforting. At this moment, something happens that only I seem to experience. Sitting there, lulled by the hum of the comfortable ceremony, I see Gene. He is approaching me directly, though his image is translucent. I can identify the shirt he is wearing as one we purchased this spring. My stomach lurches, and my pulse starts to race, marking the appearance as more than my imagination. I look around to see if anyone else seems to have seen him, but there is no sign of it.

He is smiling as he approaches me and stops just in front of me. For a second, I stare at him; and then, in a very sudden movement, he walks toward me, into and through me, and is assimilated with an audible whooshing sound. I feel the impact of his entry on my skin. I am left, blinking and rigid, afraid I am losing my mind. Emotionally, though, I am changed, stronger now, as I sense him within me. Ever the mystic and believer, I want to believe hard and smile in gratitude and joy at the touch with him. I don't even mind if I have made the event up; this is the first fortunate thing to happen to me in many days. I reel in the heady sense of his nearness. I want to turn and tell those near me, but I know better.

When I return my attention to the service, Rebecca is walking to the microphone, having bravely prepared some comments about her father for the eulogy. She approaches the microphone and blows into it three times at close range. There is a stir in the church, and those who knew Gene in his school-administrator days laugh, as they recognize what was one of Gene's eccentricities. During his years in this role as principal—or more recently, vice-principal—he would blow into the mike three times before beginning his announcements to the staff and student body. His announcements usually set off a hilarity that wasn't entirely welcomed by the teachers. Blowing into the microphone is our daughter's way of carrying on her father's tradition.

She continues in a steady, brave voice, and ends the wonderful portrait of her father with some poetry. She has chosen Wordsworth's Ode: "Intimations of Immortality from Recollections of Early Childhood," and the lines flow out over the crowd and the departed,

> *Our birth is but a sleep and a forgetting,*
> *The soul that rises with us, our life's star,*
> *Hath had elsewhere its setting,*
> *And cometh from afar;*
> *Not in entire forgetfulness,*
> *And not in utter nakedness,*
> *But trailing clouds of glory do we come,*
> *From God who is our home.*

Though nothing can bring back the hour
Of splendor in the grass, of glory in the flower,
We will grieve not, rather find
Strength in what remains behind;

She leaves the altar with such grace. I am so proud of her.

Father Mark delivers a short homily. Not knowing Gene very well, as he was a new priest in the parish at the time, he came to ask me what the theme of his remarks should be. Without hesitation, I reply that anyone who received Gene's compassion, love, and help along his path in life is honor-bound to pass that on to others who are still in this world. It is what Gene believed and lived all of his life, and it is what he would request of us. I hear this sentiment echo now in the incensed air of the church and know that Gene is happy with his final public appearance.

The time now comes to leave the cool protection of the church. We stand for the final blessing of the casket. I am still being sustained by my ghostly guest, and I feel close to him.

As we turn down the aisle, the organist in the loft above enacts another small miracle. He flips the switches of the magnificent old organ to bagpipes and begins to play "Amazing Grace." The reedy old hymn settles over the heads of all of us. We exchange looks of meaningful awareness, realizing that just a few weeks ago, Gene's friend, Freddie, was mourned with the same hymn played on bagpipes. Again, I see Gene in the birthday kitchen telling me about the ceremony.

Was there any way that I could have know then, Gene, that your leave-taking was only days away?

These thoughts take me out of the church.

We travel the six miles from the church to Hope Cemetery in a procession of silent cars. Looking back on the parade, the flags on the vehicles flutter in the steamy air. The scene in Bar Harbor returns to my mind. The flags on the parade float are mirrored here.

We enter the gates of the stately old burial grounds and wind our way up the hill to the family plot. Before their deaths, Marion and Sid installed a gravestone engraved with a bird in a nest; spring and rebirth as the theme. Gene and I have put flowers on these plots for years. I am at home here, having spent countless summers planting and tending the flowers, sitting here with my husband in silent remembering. It is a good place.

The funeral attendants have erected a small tent over the site to shade some of the crowd from the direct sun. The cosmetic devices of fake grass and flowers do not hide the deep crevice in the earth waiting to receive my husband's remains. The sun burns brutally above us, and many outside the shade of the tent feel the intense heat.

Father Mark arrives and the quiet deepens. We join hands and wait for the words to begin. One of Gene's old friends begins to sob. Automatically, I reach back through the crowd, take his hand, and pull him up with us. We, Gene's family, are shedding silent tears as well, but are so used to this by now that their progress down our faces doesn't register. Seeing this new suffering reminds us that there are others who will miss our loved one. We still do not fully understand what has happened; only time will allow the truth of this day to descend into our lives.

Gene's coffin, draped with the American flag, rests over the cleft in the earth on its hammock. The breeze sets it rocking just a little. We are surprised when soldiers come from the edge of the crowd. They position themselves at the crest of the hill and fire a twenty-one gun salute toward the lofty, white spire of the Unitarian Church at the head of Portland Road. Perfect quiet rushes in after the report. Someone solemnly blows taps. Suddenly, I am at the ceremony we witnessed in Bar Harbor only two weeks ago. The overlay of that ceremony on this one seems unreal.

Could we have known, darling; Were we being prepared for this day?

If so, we failed to read the script.

The air around us becomes so heavy we can hardly stand up. The officers step to the coffin, remove the flag, fold it ceremoniously, and briskly hand it to me. It is another Norman Rockwell tableau, and in this one, I am the widow.

The solemnity of the ceremony takes a lighter turn just now. Intending to honor Gene in a way he would have loved, Eben and Gary Archibald stole away earlier in the morning and set a fireworks display in place. As they unexpectedly set it off, a tribute to Gene's impish firework's displays on our various lawns, they frighten some and shock others. Not everyone knew this Gene. To those who didn't, this lighthearted moment seems out of keeping with the somberness of this event. To those who did know him, we knew he was laughing somewhere nearby. With this oddly juxtaposed commemoration of Gene's life, the ceremony is done; Gene is laid to rest; the coffin is lowered into the cleft that will hold his mortal remains forever.

An announcement is made that a buffet will be served at the house on Pleasant Street. People drift away, down the rutted dirt paths, to cars parked below. We, the family, stay pinned to the spot, not wanting to leave just yet. There is some talking between people who haven't seen each other in a long time, who take this opportunity, fraught with sadness though it is, to "catch up." Their light banter sounds so out of place on this spot. I wonder how they cannot feel the irony of the mundane in this brokenhearted moment.

Looking over our shoulders, we see the attendants of the cemetery waiting until we leave, ready to put everything discretely back as it was before the unkind cut was made. It is very important for them to keep the serene appearance of the space intact. The hole must be filled, the sod replaced, and the wilting flowers piled ceremoniously by the grave. This protocol is what is demanded by propriety; grief has no place here, in broad daylight.

I find myself thinking of *Our Town,* one of my favorite plays. This is a play which attempts to capture the sacred nature of everyday life in a small town. The burial of Emily, a young mother, is attended and mourned in the subdued manner prescribed by community. But later, Emily's husband comes to the graveside in the dark of night and laments beyond grief, beyond hope. Hope Cemetery is one that could be used as a set for *Our Town,* and Gene could have been its main character, with his romantic view of life and belief in the goodness of human nature. He will rest here and watch us all spin by in the lives we etch out without him. I never pass this hill again without a whispered prayer to my husband; or, for many years, without tears.

When we arrive at 22 Pleasant Street, people have preceded us. The house is crowded and noisy. The caterers laid out an excellent buffet on the dining room table, and people serve themselves, find a spot to rest, and take nourishment in one another's presence. I attempt to walk into the door of my future through little discussions and observations with the gathered. People catch up with family and friends at events like these, and I am stunned that there is anything else to talk about. I listen to the conversations, but find I don't have much left to say. Exhaustion is taking hold, along with a numbness that is not unwelcome.

Not having come to the church, my mother is waiting here, busy helping people. She gives us all an embrace and looks at us with great sympathy. We lost my father in 1988, and mother has not recovered from that blow. She is silenced by her sorrow for Rebecca, Eben, and me, and she cannot find words to express herself. In the years of her life left to live, she is to become my sidekick. Both widows now, we share an experience that is very deep and precious.

The afternoon passes swiftly, full of conversations and condolences. The mood of the funeral changes into a party atmosphere, and I, along with the children and close family, are distanced by this distraction from the reason everyone is in our house this day. By evening, the crowd thins. the children are on the deck with a group of their friends; I am on the front porch with some high school chums who made the trip from Rumford. My heart is filled with their caring; we revert to old habits together, like smoking cigarettes and drinking wine.

Then, I am alone inside the darkening house. Though some are still outside, left to talk softly, I choose to sit quietly inside. The hubbub of the day calms, and at the center of my heart, I discover a glowing coal of pain. A frenzy of fear spreads out from this center like an alarm; I begin to search for escape. At that moment, a neighbor comes to sit with me for a short while. As a professional counselor, she offers me words that make a difference then; words that I hold onto through the intervening years. She tells me that all of the mourners here today have genuine sympathy for me and the family and for Gene. However, very few of them really believe they will ever have to experience the same thing. Then she reminds me that Gene's fate is *our* fate; it is the human condition. Even though he died earlier than anyone wanted for him, he experienced nothing that all of us won't experience in our own lives at our own times. Somehow, her words help for the moment; they help to ease the feelings of punishment this death has brought.

With those words ringing in my head, I leave the house and sorrow behind and climb the stairs to sleep, but first, I go to the dresser to find the penny from the dream on the altar of relics I have constructed from our lives. I hold it and ask for help in understanding what has happened. That is my last prayer on the day of prayers; the day we lay my dear Gene to eternal rest.

July 22ND, AND BEYOND

The aftermath of such a traumatic death is much worse than the period of activity and ritual marking the event. The silence and immensity of space in the new life is huge, and is like nothing anyone could imagine. Every pathway to meaning laid down in my life as wife and friend to my husband disappears like a contrail in the sky, and I am lost.

Under a Mean Moon

like two children
in that dense wood
we have lost each other.

we let go of hands
and the mean trees and spiky moon
cast shadows and played games
with us.

now, I walk this forest
in the windy night of being
alone,
and look for crumbs
that shine out of the dark
to lead me to you,

but they are scattered and
tangled in the web of wind.

I see them in places, though,
the crumbs,
hieroglyphics of when you were here.
they lead me round and round
searching for you
though you have gone missing for a long night
and I am not so nimble any more.
I tire and sit by the roadside
forgetting why I am in these woods
and what I would find.

the road home has closed up.
the sweet scent of sacrifice is on the air
that wafts in night's breeze.
there is powerful magic in
this dark,
I cower in the heart of the forest
and fear this place.

I must steal away silently
and attract no notice
no matter what is framed
in the glowing windows
above my sight.

The ordinary little town of Kennebunk becomes a field of emotional landmines. Route One, as it passes the cemetery on the hill, is to be avoided at all costs. It is almost impossible to keep the car moving beyond the cemetery entrance, and often, I turn in to sit and weep. I put a penny on the marker stone recently installed by the U.S. Army. I plant flowers, sit, and talk endlessly to the wind.

The supermarket, once friendly and full of possibility, has become the black hole of despair. I implode halfway through my first shopping attempt; there is nothing to buy, no dinners to prepare, and nothing I want. The shelves that once called out to me with delightful possibility in the veneer of casseroles, vegetables, and desserts hold only blank reminders of that life now. I am not eating; the thought of cooking makes me ill. I have lost enough weight for neighbors to comment; one making a joke about my shorts falling off if I don't change my ways.

Among the other landmines to explode are the casual and close relationships I once kept in easy, supportive reach. When I finally venture out in public a few weeks after the funeral, at a play I attend, in the drugstore, or other public settings, I am aware of people looking at me and quickly turning away in a vain attempt to pretend that they haven't looked into the face of my grief. I feel surprise and pain when this first happens, and it does not make matters easier. Averted eyes, a lack of greeting, and the fear I find in others who come face-to-face with me becomes a common experience, driving me deeper into an experience of isolation.

Since that time, I have learned this response is really about the fear of causing the bereaved anymore pain, and about the uncertainty of what to say in the wake of such events. After my experiences, it has become a practice to approach someone in grief and offer my sorrow and concern in plain words. As I lived through the first days following Gene's death, this was what helped me. I am thankful to friends who braved their own fears to offer recognition and concern to me.

At first, the daily chores and pleasures that were a part of the beloved, old life—the template for action that filled sunrise to sundown—are erased. I sit on my couch in the family room; I sit in the center of the couch, in the center of a whirling vortex of loneliness, and I wait, although I could not tell you what I was waiting for. When I can't wait any longer, I go to the car and begin to drive the area that used to be familiar to me. I go to Saco and Biddeford, Wells, Ogunquit; everywhere I go, there are landmarks of the past. At a certain point, the realization of what has happened becomes too much to bear, and within the secure interior of my car, I scream at the top of my lungs. I scream and scream, until I am tired enough to go home and fall asleep.

Rebecca and Ahmet return to Middlebury to pick up the shards of their life there.

The program administrators allow my daughter to continue in her program, in spite of the time she has lost and the difficulty she has concentrating on her work there. In September, she will move to Princeton, New Jersey, and begin work on a Ph.D. in French. Her father was so proud of his daughter, and he loved his trips into her world of academe. I will help them move by driving their car to Princeton behind the loaded moving van. There are so many ways and so many days, Gene is missed.

Eben is not returning to college this fall. Gene hesitantly agreed to a year off for his son before the events of the last month transpired. I am grateful to have him here, though we both move through the house in quiet sadness. I appreciate the focus caring for him provides. We go to mass in Biddeford on the first Sunday after the funeral. While in the church, the funeral replays itself in my mind. I end up weeping quietly through most of the service. After mass, we walk together from Pleasant Street, through the sunny little town, to the new grave on the hill. The visit is awkward. We cannot believe that our beloved's earthly body is here. The thought of him being beneath the earth of this place is incomprehensible, yet we must learn to believe it is true. *Is that ever possible?*

We walk home in silence.

Slowly, life begins to thrum to the beat of completing the many little needs of the day: making the bed, sweeping the kitchen, cutting the grass, and cooking food that doesn't always get eaten. It seems that finding and following the thread of activity is the only way I get to sleep and find relief from this new and terribly foreign way of life.

JULY 25ᵀᴴ, 1994

It is late. I am attempting to read, but I am drowsy. I am waiting to hear Eben come home before giving in to sleep. I hear him walk noisily through the downstairs, turning off lights, and coming to the second floor. He calls goodnight to me on his way up to his attic bedroom. I answer good night, rest my head on the pillows behind me, and wait for sleep to find me.

Suddenly, Gene is with me. He is in a large room, much like a ballroom, and comes to the edge of it, leaning into my room. I am conscious of what he is wearing, his khakis again, and this time, his navy-blue, short-sleeved shirt. He waves to me with the flat-palmed wave he used all of his life. He is smiling, and he looks wonderful. He speaks to me, but he doesn't use words to speak. It is a communication of thought.

"Come over here," he says. Immediately, I feel a surge of warm, buzzing waves ride through my whole body. He is hugging me. Ecstasy bounds up through me, and I glow in this warmth. I am not thinking now, just feeling, and I don't have anything to say to him. He then delivers a message that, in retrospect, will cause me pain: "Now you have to live for yourself."

I don't understand why he is saying this. Hasn't he come back to me? Buoyed up by his visit, I smile into his face again. There is no doubt in my mind that he is here, and that is enough, just now, for me. He waves again, smiling directly into my eyes, then fades away and is gone. I fall asleep holding to the image, not fully aware of the message, just happy with the surge of contact.

When I wake, the memory is still with me. For the moment, joy is mine. He was here, I know that deeply. As the import of his message comes clear, the smile on my lips fades. Perhaps I have seen the last of that dear face. We had promised each other to attempt to return from death and report about the process. Was this what he was doing, getting back to me? His appearance didn't promise anything more. He advised me to go on without him; I could see by his demeanor that, wherever he is, he is not unhappy without me. I am disheartened by these ideas, but—and I am getting proficient in this—I try not to focus on them just now.

I arrive at an aerobics class in Saco that morning and join my family there. John, Monica, and Ted are in the same class. I begin talking ecstatically about the visit, as if it were the most usual thing in the world. Looking back to that day, I wonder what it must have been like for them to have their newly widowed sister describe her dead husband's final spiritual embrace. I am so elated to have had such an experience that I become careless about what others can tolerate. I see their faces fall with sympathy, but also, I see that they don't understand. I stop talking.

The high of this event soon gives way to great weight as I realize that this visit was a final gesture for all time. It is too enormous a truth for me to accept, and I turn away from it, putting it away in some part of my mind that I might visit later.

After this mystical event, pennies begin to rain down from everywhere. I have the "shower" penny safely tucked away for the rest of my life in a small cedar box Gene bought for me on a trip to Florida a few springs earlier. Now pennies appear in my bed; in my slippers; under wine glasses that have been put, cup down, on the sideboard; on the sidewalk as I go out into the world for errands; and later in my life, one appears under the chair I am sitting on as I open the first photograph of our grandchild on my computer in May of 2004. Gene has become the dispenser of pennies from the world beyond.

Often, friends and family call to tell me of the pennies that appear in their lives as well, on airplane seats after three hours in flight; in closets not used for years; and in other impossible places. I feel blessed by each and every penny, and I know that, in the timeless place my husband resides now, he is still sending me love in the words of the first message from so long ago. *"Look for pennies in strange places,"* they told us, and I find them in strange places everywhere.

I remember also the question, *"Is there life after death?"* The pennies offer an answer.

AUGUST, 1994

Now it is August, and an early dusk is settling on the house and yard. I sit on the deck, watching the quiet descent of the end of the day. In the kitchen behind the glass doors that lead out to the deck, pizzas cool on the stovetop. They are not *just* pizzas; they are testimonies to the hundreds of pizzas I have made on Sunday and Friday nights, and to the celebration of our family's being together: homemade crust, whole-wheat and white, hand-seasoned sauce, and an inventive variety of cheeses and toppings. The smell is enticing and warming. It drifts out, onto the deck, in the evening breeze.

There is a deep tension within me, and I continue to sit, although the pizzas are getting cold as sin. I wait. From deep within me, I feel sure that this is the night *he* will call. In my heart and mind, I know all the relevant details. I know that my husband had a stroke; I know he is gone. A protective layer of shock insulates me, and though I *know* he is dead, I can't understand why he doesn't at least *call*. His clothes are still in the closet upstairs, although his terrycloth bathrobe and pajamas have disappeared, carried away by the children in an attempt to make things easier for me, I am sure.

Tonight, the pizza is a trigger of some sort. I have made three large pies, more than Eben and I can possibly eat…and Eben and I are the only ones home. The pizzas wait. In some perfectly lucid way, I wait for Gene to come home to dinner, as he has for twenty-four years. He *will* call. As a matter of fact, I get angry that he hasn't called yet. *Where is he?* The question rises in my throat and chokes my breathing, deepening the tension.

Where on the face of this earth is this man? The man who would never, in any circumstance, let me down willingly? The man so devoted, he would ride through blizzards no one else dared, just to have dinner with me? Where is he?

I wait, listening for the phone to ring, and finally, it does. In one leap, I am in the kitchen, and I grab the receiver to holler a hello. I wait to hear his sweet voice with an apology for leaving me for so long. The voice I hear is that of a friend, calling to check on me. The disappointment in my voice soon turns to embarrassingly deep sobs that scare the hell out of the caller. Not able to explain, I hang up, go back to the deck, and sit. The pizzas get very cold, and I don't care that night, or for many nights. Sometimes, if I let myself, I could still not care.

December 14ᵗʰ, 2004

And again, I am waiting at death's door. It is my mother. A window frames the dancing light on this December afternoon. Dark pines and cedars, a Greek chorus, thrash and wail, reaching to hold the day in place, but it slips past, as surely as the woman beside me will soon slip away. She is my faithful, courageous mother in the last, unimaginable hours of her strong and holy life.

All of this day, a single crow is weaving his darkness in the trees; a black ribbon stitching time and light together into one hour, and then the next, as I watch and wait. These cruel hours accumulate, each one more urgent than the last. And, when my mother's life comes to its end, night will fall, and the crow will complete his prophesy.

lost in Oz
for Ida

The girl has been away from home for so long,
her memory is a thin dress.
now and then, though, the
desire for return comes, and
she would trade in this
make believe world
for the memory of shadows
before the dream.

the companion to her on that road,
I have played all the parts,
coward as a lion,
unthinking straw man
and heartless tin man,
but I have kept on, steady and true,
through it all.

long ago, the good witch told her
that she could always go home,
but she stayed
to keep company those who needed her
blue guidance.

tonight, the heels of her
red slippers tremble
and reach for each other.
how many taps will it take,
three?
there's no place like home,
there's no place like home

what does magic look like?

He is only one crow. I am not foolish enough to count him. He calls in his piercing caw for me to acknowledge him, but I refuse; I count, instead, the bursts of oxygen from the instrument holding my mother here, or I count the beads on my rosary while I travel the well-trod mystical labyrinth. *I will not count a single crow; I dare not.*

JANUARY, 2006

Two black crows have swooped into the deepening white of the front yard. I live here in the woods of Maine now. The dark green of pines and cedars, held up by the gray and black of trunks and limbs, support the falling, white snow with their color. Two crows—*two crows, joy*—are pecking at what is left of the garden for this year, the garden that is disappearing underneath the white tide; sunflower seeds, dried asparagus ferns, whatever they can find that will provide some warmth in this cold.

They stride the land of our home like it is theirs, and today, it is. No one will shoo them away. Watching them, I have counted them unaware. It is very quiet in this moment; the snow brings the silence of space as it descends on the garden in the center of the woods.

tableau

we are at the center
you and I,
what was it…
a grotto in deep woods
delicate, young, trees
grow around us,
reaching over our heads
fondly.

and the light,
it is kind and warm
rising from nowhere
foaming around us
into the dawning sky
like snow filling the air.
we are embraced
in its blessing.

deer stand
a small distance apart.
their glossy radiance pulses
with large eyed-interest;
they offer us this
to wear as a cloak.
we stand there together,
awed by the silent procession
of night, feeling
the music of stars through our skin,
waiting,
in that holy place.

I live in this place now. I have earned it. The sudden pain of our parting has been cauterized and is healing; bringing the enhanced command of strength to the edges of what was the wound. No one who has experienced such a death can ever claim to be healed. The day will never come when I brush my hands together and dismiss the experience as over. Rather, I forever move away from the point of explosion in my past; the point where I broke apart at the center. But like infinity, I learn to divide the eclipse of the experience—first in half, then in quarters, and so on, and so on—but never will I come to zero. The gift has been given and received;

I am forever changed. And though I am disfigured in many ways, acting my part in human affairs, I see that my vision of the world is a very privileged perspective, achieved at great price; one that encourages me to hold the hands of compassion out to all and to see with eyes of forgiveness.

In all acts of farewell, I now look directly into the eyes of the person I am leaving, or the person leaving me. I look and speak directly and strongly, tell them I love them, and attempt to hold some of their precious energy within my heart as we part. I know how long it can be until we see each other again. And if, by some accident of time, I cannot say goodbye and offer love in the flesh, I whisper my love on the wind and send it to them in spirit.

The question of what really matters in life has an answer. What really matters is unqualified love and joyous support, open communication, deep caring, and sincere appreciation for the people with whom we live and share the great mystery of life.

To have those simple, ordinary moments of my life with Gene back again, to change the direction that my life took the summer of 1994; that is impossible…but to understand and express the deep love and gratitude that is in my heart for his gift of himself to me in our lives, that is the miracle. There are these miracles in every life, waiting to be discovered at the heart.

And beyond that discovery, the miracle is to recognize that the people I live life with now, both those I meet randomly and those companions close on my path, are there to offer to me the opportunity to love, to enjoy, to forgive, to appreciate, to support, to teach, and to learn from, in every waking moment. My prayer is to see and to understand that I am blessed by them in every moment of my life.

Saturday, April, 1994

It is a raw, spring day. The Maine variety of gray skies and scudding clouds, combined with cold temperatures, makes it necessary to get out of the house or go crazy waiting to be released from winter. We board the Nissan van we love so much and head up the Maine coast to Brunswick, anxious to escape the interstate for more rural roads, then, on to Bath, and breaking free on the little road out to Small Point Beach and the cold Atlantic beyond.

Along the way, we see many robins and geese, reassurances that spring is really here, though it is not flaunting itself yet, as it often does not in Maine. The cold stays out of the car as we fill the cab with comfortable heat. We tune in a public radio station we have listened to for years; the "Click and Clack" morning tirade on just now. When we arrive on the island, it is noon; still, we add scarves and gloves against the wind blowing in from the sea. We see fog fragments streaming along in the gale. There are sporadic rain showers that make the mood complete; Maine in the spring!

We pass over a long road that separates the island campsites from the parking lot and store. They are all boarded up now; there appears to be no one here but us and the deer. Pampas grass along the road blows in the wind, making a hypnotic clicking sound as we stride along in our boots. This marsh grass is the homeland of hundreds of red-winged blackbirds in the summer sun, but just now, the wind has built a nest here and is in full occupancy. The dancing fronds keep time with the brisk, cold, ocean breeze.

We reach the upswing of the road to the cliff-side campsites where we camped on many memorable summers. Just recovering from having a bout with the flu, I feel the full effect of energy draining from my body. A sudden tiredness overtakes me, and I express a wish to rest in the granite outcroppings along the road that are protected from the wind.

I encourage Gene to continue without me; I will wait here, with some reading I have brought, until he returns. He protests a little, but soon sees that I am really not up to the hike, and am better off resting. In fact, I look forward to the quiet meditation I might find in such a beautiful natural refuge. We find a place out of the wind for me, a place from which a long expanse of the road he will travel is visible. Settling in, I take out a book I stuffed in my pocket and agree that I will rest to be ready for more walking when he returns.

Gene is especially tender just now, making sure I am warm and comfortable, fussing uncharacteristically over me. Then he kisses me goodbye and continues on his way, promising to return within the hour. He sets off on the path ahead, turning to wave often as he recedes into the distance and finally drops out of my sight.

I turn to my reading, comfortable and thankful to be able to let enough energy pool in my body to get me back to the car. I doze a little, but something wakes me up. Not knowing where I am for a moment, I feel anxiety rise in my blood. I sit up quickly and look around; my breath is short. But as I search the landscape for something familiar, I see Gene at a far distance, on top of one of the many rock outcroppings stretching along the edge of the sea. He shades his eyes, looking for me. At first, a fear surges. He is so far from me. Leaping and climbing to the top of the rock nearby. I begin to wave frantically. I wave and wave, and finally, he sees me and waves back. I don't know how long we stand waving, but it is a happy moment, and—though we never talk about it on the way home—it is also a curiously illuminating one. From this distance in time, it appears a harbinger of things to come.

In the aftermath of his swift departure, this moment returns many times to warm my heart. In it, there is a brief glimpse of his exit from the life we treasured. Within it, there is also a promise: the promise that he is just ahead of me on the path. He can still see me behind him, and I can find him on the edge of the sea, looking for me, waiting for me to catch up.

And now, he is not alone. My mother has joined him since his leaving, and of course, the path to that place is well-trod. When I achieve his path, when I find him, he will turn his head as he did that day and wave me on. Love will be in his smile; love and a welcome to his new world.

> *I will look for you there,*
> *when the ferryman comes for me.*
> *I will call your name from the boat,*
> *I will ask it as a blessing*
> *begging entrance to your new world.*

ferryman, ferryman

pleasant street curves
up and away from town
following rivers of the past
rising to a ridge
and flowing out...

beneath, flowing with the asphalt,
runs a shadow river,
a silent, cold, coursing
secret as a hidden moon.
the ferryman mounts his bark,
and no one marks the departure.

beneath the pleasant street
dark waters swirl
below the slow footsteps
of Sunday afternoons
and rushing school mornings,
far beneath the mounds of cold snow
and thirsty roots of trees-
under the fire-hearted homes
of friends
the river Styx roils.

this night, the hidden moon
rises in your eyes
you are with him already
looking away from me,
feel him put out into the current,
the strong, swift, sure slide of
black water tugs
you away from me
and here
and now
and you go without hesitation.

this night,
you are still dying in the driveway.
I run to shield myself
from your sudden and heartless departure
in the now empty house.

the weekend melts
in the sink where I have thrown it:
its frozen moisture pools and puddles
and drips down the deep drain
in long, echoing drops
like music

and the ferryman poles his passenger
to the river Styx
flowing gently,
silently,
endlessly
into that other river,
Lethe,
its waters reflecting the sky in perfect
circle, seamless and serene.

I will look for you there
when the ferryman comes for me.
I will call your name from the boat,
I will ask it as a blessing
begging entrance to your new world.

About the Author

Cynthia Fraser Graves is the keeper of the details of the life and death events recounted in Never Count Crow. Her previously self- published work is *eyes like jewels*, a poetry collection, and she is presently at work on a novel titled *Dusk on Route One*. Fraser Graves taught English for three decades before retiring in 2000 to write full-time from her home on the southern Maine Coast. She is the recipient of a first prize in Nonfiction from the 2006 Writer's Conference at Ocean Park, Maine.